# *The* VIRGINIA CONTINENTAL LINE *in the* REVOLUTION'S SOUTHERN CAMPAIGNS

JOHN C. SETTLE

THE History PRESS

Published by The History Press
An imprint of Arcadia Publishing
Charleston, SC
www.historypress.com



First published 2025

Manufactured in the United States

ISBN 9781467157902

Library of Congress Control Number: 2025931886

*To the memory of the officers and men of the Virginia Continental Line who served throughout the American Revolution.*

# CONTENTS

# ACKNOWLEDGEMENTS

There are many people I would like to thank for their support with this book. I would like to express my thanks to my father, Lyle Settle, and my sister, Katie, for their continuing support throughout this long project. Thank you to my mother, Amanda, for her support and assistance on our road trip to retrieve pictures of different battles across North and South Carolina. I would also like to express gratitude to my good friend Noah Crawford, who through countless phone calls and road trips assisted in providing insight and a second pair of eyes to the writing, as well as moral support to the writer. I would also acknowledge my coworkers from Colonial Williamsburg, Nandua Middle School and Powhatan Middle School who offered moral support and academic advice through this process, as well as other friends who supported me over the years.

# INTRODUCTION

In September 1780, Lewis Griffin was just a few weeks from his seventeenth birthday. He went with a neighbor from Halifax County, Virginia, to take tobacco to Petersburg. In Petersburg, Lewis met his brother Griffin, who was in service with the Virginia Continentals there. Griffin, who was Lewis' senior by fifteen years, tried to recruit his brother into the army. Lewis gave in to his brother's persuasion and enlisted for eighteen months, with the understanding that he would only be required to remain in Petersburg with his brother to guard the public magazine and horses there.[1] This lasted for about three months; then Lewis, his brother and ten others were marched from Petersburg to Chesterfield Courthouse on the order of the Baron de Steuben and formed into a company under Captain James Culbertson. Despite what Lewis was told when he enlisted, he was marched out of Virginia into North Carolina with a new battalion of Virginia Continentals. They were uniformed in blue jackets and later, in the camps, were called "the regiment of Hell-fired-blues of the Virginia Line."[2] Their reputation in the coming campaigns would reinforce the name.

Following the capture of Charleston and the disaster at Waxhaws in the spring of 1780, the ranks of the Virginia Continental Line had to be filled and new battalions organized to take the field again. This proved to be difficult. These organizations were not the same as the original fifteen regiments raised in the early years of the Revolution. The military fever that had filled the ranks of the early Virginia Line had long died out with disease and suffering and on battlefields like Brandywine and Germantown. Many of the most experienced officers (including two generals) were now prisoners of war. The shortage of officers in general was felt in the early stages of the late war period in Virginia. The loss of experienced soldiers was felt not only in the officer corps but in the ranks as well. Over 1,300 men were now prisoners of war, and many had refused to reenlist after their enlistments expired early in 1780. The few veterans of the Virginia Continental Line who remained uncaptured became the nucleus of the companies and battalions to be formed in the coming months. Five years of war had taken its toll on Virginia. Inflation, a seemingly never-ending war and disasters in the South damaged the will of Virginians, whether they supported the war or not. War weariness and horrifying stories from veterans who returned home deterred recruits from joining the Continental Army. With the ranks thin and only a trickle of recruits coming in, the state government implemented a draft to strengthen the Virginia Line.

Commanders like Peter Muhlenberg and the Baron de Steuben cobbled together these old veterans, new volunteers, drafted men and substitutes into companies and battalions. After receiving only some of the most basic equipment, they were sent into the field to fight the enemy in the Carolinas and in Virginia itself. Often these men went without, and the phrase "literally naked" appeared in many letters from the officers in relation to the appearance of their men. A soldier would receive a pair of stockings but no shoes, and when the socks wore out, he received his shoes! Virginia, which had already sent many supplies over the past five years, strained to supply not only the Virginia troops but also the Southern Army in the Carolinas. Unlike the early war regiments, the companies were formed not by regions but by whoever was at one location at any given time. This led to men from all over Virginia being grouped with complete strangers, led by officers who were often strangers as well. Despite the promise of a bounty and monthly pay, very few of these men received pay during their subsequent service. Despite the shortages and hardships, battalions were formed and went into the field after being trained by Steuben, the famed Drillmaster of Valley Forge.

Some of these troops went down south to serve with General Nathanael Greene. Guilford Courthouse became the proving ground for the Virginians, who held their ground and served as the rear guard for the army. Later, they lived up to their reputation at places like Hobkirk Hill and Ninety-Six. They were praised by General Greene for breaking the British line at the Battle of Eutaw Springs, though their ranks were thinned by casualties. In Virginia, Continental troops fought alongside state troops and militia as they tried to

Alonzo Chappel, *Siege of Charleston* (1862). *Prints, Drawings and Watercolors from the Anne S.K. Brown Military Collection, Brown Digital Repository, Brown University.*

defend their home. They marched hundreds of miles and took part in the Siege of Yorktown. The remainder of the war was spent down south, where the Virginians helped to keep British forces off-balance and took part in the operations to retake Savannah and Charleston. Their "hell-fired" reputation was not exclusive to the battlefield. Resistance in the ranks to mistreatment and the lack of supplies and pay was not unusual in the Virginia Line. When men went without shoes and the quartermaster was slow to respond, some officers broke into the stores and took shoes for their men. Some men were arrested for complaining too loudly when issued rotten meat, and nearly half a battalion rose up to free them from the blockhouse. Officers refused to march when ordered south due to tardy pay. Even when pressured by General George Washington to march, the enlisted men resisted, and some had to be beaten to march south without pay or proper clothing.

Much of the Virginia Line's service in the late period of the American Revolution has been forgotten. What has been written down contains many errors and misunderstandings regarding the nature of the battalions and their service. In 1968, John Robert Sellers wrote his doctoral dissertation on the history of the Virginia Line, but he admitted that the Virginia Line was

*Left*: Regulars Monument at Guilford Courthouse National Military Park. *Author's collection.*

*Opposite*: Nathanael Greene Monument at Guilford Courthouse National Military Park. *Author's collection.*

"too large a subject to be covered in a dissertation of reasonable length."[3] His dissertation ended with Charleston and Waxhaws. Sellers admitted to wanting to write a more detailed history of the Virginia Line, to include the story of the organization after Charleston. Ten years later, Sellers did publish a study on the Virginia Line including the post-Charleston period, but unlike his nearly four-hundred-page dissertation, his book *The Virginia Continental Line* is only eighty-four pages, of which nine cover the late war period. These nine pages offer only a glimpse into the service of the Virginia Line, and though Sellers' is one of a handful of books on Virginia Continental troops during the Revolution and gives an overview of the Virginians, it is not without limitations. Other books have been written on officers of the Virginia Line, with at least one book for nearly all the Virginia generals, and two books written for the early war regiments.

The Virginia Line, despite its record, has not had the same publicity as other units during the Revolution. During the research for this book, I found that the Maryland Line and the Delaware Regiment were often mentioned in the southern campaigns and always overshadowed the Virginia troops.

The Virginians fought right alongside these troops, yet when one reads the secondary accounts of battles such as Cowpens, Guilford Courthouse or Hobkirk Hill, one finds that the Virginians are nearly forgotten or misunderstood. In Patrick O'Donnell's *Washington's Immortals*, which describes the history of the Maryland Line throughout the entire Revolution, the credit is often given almost entirely to the Marylanders, with little to no mention of the Virginians fighting by their side. A history of the Battle of Guilford Courthouse composed by the Guilford Battle Ground Company in 1893 completely omits the presence of the Virginia Continentals and only includes them in one map.[4] In contrast, the same history states that the Marylanders and Delawarians "covered themselves in immortal glory."[5] This is not to say that the Marylanders or the Delaware Regiment do not deserve credit for their service—but in the recognition of that service, those Virginians were forgotten. The complexity of the Virginia battalions and the different geographic locations of the primary sources only made the service records harder to further document, and so they were forgotten to the extent that their participation in certain battles is unknown.

It is the hope of the author that this book will give a voice to those who many have forgotten—through their recollections of their service in letters after the war and their pension applications in the early nineteenth century, when they were finally offered an avenue to tell their story. Often, in the course of submitting these applications, veterans of the battalions were able to locate old comrades, and they testified to each other's service, thus substantiating each other's stories. No longer strangers as before, when they were recruits, these old soldiers now relied on each other to give testimony about experiences that many others did not know of or understand. When death took the last of the veterans, their story was forgotten again. On July 3, 1915, a crowd gathered for the dedication of the Nathanael Greene Monument on the Guilford Courthouse battlefield. In the modern day, visitors to the Guilford Courthouse National Military Park will see this impressive monument, surrounded by other monuments and the graves of two signers of the Declaration of Independence. Located on the front of the monument, a plaque commemorates the service of the regulars and militiamen who fought in the battle. The first half of the plaque states the importance of the Battle of Guilford Courthouse, while the second half is dedicated to the officers and men. One line from the plaque, though generalized to all the troops who fought there, can be applied to the Virginia Continental Line after 1780 and best summarizes the goal of this book: "They neither need defense nor eulogy but only just recognition."

## Chapter 1

# OFFICERS AND MEN OF THE VIRGINIA LINE, 1780–83

The officers and men of the Virginia Continental Line were unique individuals. The officers were mostly veterans, who had led men into battle many times in battles in the northern theater of the Revolution. The enlisted men exemplified the various backgrounds of Virginians in the last quarter of the eighteenth century. Motivations for enlisting varied from soldier to soldier, from political to economic to personal reasons. To understand the service and actions of the Virginia Line in the last part of the Revolution, one must understand the backgrounds of the officers and men.

## General and Field Officers of the Virginia Line

Brigadier General John Peter Gabriel Muhlenberg was a thirty-four-year-old veteran of four years by the spring of 1780. He began the Revolution as the commissioned colonel of the Eighth Virginia Regiment, which was raised from men within the Shenandoah Valley, where Muhlenberg had been a preacher before the Revolution.[6] After spending only a few months in Suffolk, the Eighth Virginia went with Major General Charles Lee to South Carolina, where it was present during the Battle of Sullivan's Island in June 1776. The Virginians suffered severely from disease and the heat of South Carolina, and nearly half of the regiment died before it was ordered back to Virginia in August 1776, though many of the sick men were left in South Carolina until they recovered.[7]

After recruiting to replenish his regiment, Muhlenberg was promoted to brigadier general and given command of a brigade consisting of the First, Fifth, Ninth and Thirteenth Virginia Regiments and the Eighth Maryland Regiment (known as the German Battalion).[8] The brigade, called the First Virginia Brigade, fought in the division commanded by Major General Nathanael Greene. After fighting at the Battle of Brandywine, Muhlenberg commanded Greene's division at Germantown, where his old brigade advanced further into the British camps than other American unit, but not without cost. The Ninth Virginia Regiment pushed forward too far and was captured, along with portions of the Sixth and Eighth Virginia Regiments.

After the winter at Valley Forge, Muhlenberg still commanded his shrunken First Virginia Brigade. A few recruits from the Ninth Virginia were added to the depleted First and Fifth Virginia Regiments and consolidated into one regiment for the 1778 campaign. The First and Second Virginia State Regiments had been added to his brigade, though it was still understrength. Muhlenberg was present at Monmouth Courthouse, and his brigade spent most of the day marching to the battlefield and was in reserve during the attack on Stony Point, New York, in July 1779.[9] As the Virginians marched south in January 1780, General Muhlenberg was left in Philadelphia while General William Woodford led the remainder of the Virginia Line to Charleston. Muhlenberg considered resigning to return home, but Congress instead assigned him to go take command of the recruiting service in Virginia. Muhlenberg arrived in Richmond, Virginia, and reported directly to Governor Jefferson.[10]

Brigadier General Daniel Morgan was one of the most famous Virginia officers during the American Revolution. A rifleman and veteran of the French and Indian War from Frederick County, Morgan was one of the first to raise a company of riflemen for Continental service in the summer of 1775. He was captured during the unsuccessful invasion of Canada and returned to service over a year later as the colonel of the Eleventh Virginia Regiment.[11] He was best known for his command of a regiment of riflemen raised by Washington in the summer of 1777. His riflemen proved effective as light infantry in New Jersey, where Morgan was praised by Washington. Morgan's riflemen were then sent north and fought admirably in the Saratoga Campaign under General Horatio Gates. Morgan's riflemen rejoined Washington's army outside of Philadelphia in November 1777. Throughout 1778, his riflemen served as part of Washington's light infantry.

By the spring of 1780, Morgan was no longer active with the army. He was repeatedly passed over for promotion in favor of generals who had less

*Left*: Major General Peter Muhlenberg. *Miriam and Ira D. Wallach Division of Art, Prints and Photographs: Print Collection, New York Public Library Digital Collections.*

*Right*: Brigadier General D. Morgan. *Miriam and Ira D. Wallach Division of Art, Prints and Photographs: Print Collection, New York Public Library Digital Collections.*

combat experience but more political connections. His beloved rifle corps was broken up in the summer of 1778, and he returned to command the Seventh Virginia. Morgan hoped for promotion to brigadier and command of the new light infantry corps Washington had formed in 1778 but was passed over in favor of fellow Virginian Charles Scott. When Scott went to Virginia to recruit in the spring of 1779, Morgan again was passed over, this time in favor of General Anthony Wayne. The lack of promotions, along with pain in his legs and back from continuous service, caused Morgan to submit his resignation on June 30, 1779, and he returned to his home in Frederick County.[12] The full resignation was not accepted; he was permitted to return home on extended furlough until either General Washington or Congress ordered him to return.

On June 14, 1780, Congress ordered Morgan to return to service and report directly to General Horatio Gates.[13] A month later, Morgan's name was submitted for promotion to brigadier general. Morgan departed

Richmond on September 20, 1780, and assumed command of the light infantry of the Southern Army.[14] On October 13, he finally received his promotion to brigadier general.[15]

Colonel Abraham Buford, like Morgan, had been in military service since the beginning of the war. Born and raised in Culpeper County, Buford began the war as a captain in the Culpeper Minute Battalion and fought in one of the first engagements in Virginia, at Hampton, in October 1775. He was again engaged at the victory at Great Bridge in December 1775.[16] In November 1776, his company was disbanded, and Buford was appointed major of the newly formed Fourteenth Virginia Regiment on November 13.[17] His time with the regiment was short, as on April 1, 1777, he was appointed lieutenant colonel of the Fifth Virginia Regiment. Buford was present with the regiment at Brandywine and Germantown. In May 1778, he was promoted to colonel and transferred to command the Eleventh Virginia Regiment.

Following the Virginia Line's reorganization at White Plains in the fall of 1778, Buford was sent in the winter to gather new recruits from Virginia and march them to New Jersey. The fall of Savannah and the British threat to Charleston changed his destination. He was assigned to the command of General Charles Scott at Fredericksburg in May 1779 and commanded a battalion of Virginia Continentals during the Mathew-Collier Raid.[18] In June, Buford and his men were marched to Petersburg, where they were organized into detachments to be sent south.[19] Buford was given command of what is referred to as the Third Virginia Detachment, along with Lieutenant Colonel Robert Ballard and Major Thomas Ridley.

Lack of clothing, mostly shirts and shoes, prevented the men under Colonel Buford from marching south. Buford worked hard to get his men supplies, making several trips to Williamsburg to convince Governor Jefferson and the General Assembly to grant supplies and money.[20] Buford's Third Virginia Detachment was the last of the three detachments to leave Virginia in April 1780. The detachment did not reach Charleston in time, and at Waxhaws, South Carolina, it met its fate, decimated in a matter of minutes. Buford survived the battle, but the massacre of his Virginians after their surrender there became the subject of controversy and a rallying cry for southerners. Despite debates about the alleged "massacre," Buford and his survivors marched back to Virginia to form the nucleus of the Virginia Line.

Colonel William Davies was a lawyer from Norfolk, Virginia. He was commissioned as captain of the First Virginia Regiment in October 1775 and marched north with the regiment in August 1776.[21] He was captured at Fort Washington in November 1776 and remained a prisoner of war for two months. While imprisoned, he was appointed major of the Seventh Virginia Regiment, and on February 21, 1777, he was commissioned as lieutenant colonel of the Fourteenth Virginia Regiment.

Davies proved himself a capable officer both on the battlefield and in the camp. Before his capture at Fort Washington, he had served as deputy muster master general of the Flying Camp in New Jersey.[22] The Fourteenth Virginia was noted for good conduct at both Brandywine and Germantown. At Valley Forge, Davies was one of the original five sub-inspectors chosen by the Baron de Steuben. His duty as sub-inspector was to learn the new manual developed by the baron and train the troops of Washington's army in the new drill. He was promoted to colonel in March 1778 and remained in nominal command of the Fourteenth Virginia (reorganized as the Tenth Virginia at White Plains in September 1778), but his duties as sub-inspector kept him away from the regiment.

Like many other field officers in the winter of 1780, Colonel Davies returned to Virginia on furlough. While he was at home, the Virginia Line was ordered south, and General Washington ordered Davies to rejoin the Virginia Line when it arrived in Virginia, resume his duties as sub-inspector and possibly return to field command of his regiment.[23] Davies joined the troops at Petersburg, where he found General Woodford, who, because of his dislike for Davies, had appointed Colonel Samuel Cabell sub-inspector over Davies.[24] Davies was not without his conflicts; he had written to a friend about his hatred for General Woodford, going back to the burning and looting of Norfolk, where Davies had lost much of his property.[25] Davies, now without a regiment and his position as sub-inspector, applied to Washington for an assignment. Washington responded by ordering him to remain in Virginia to assist Muhlenberg in recruiting and organizing troops to be sent south.[26] Thus, Davies remained in Virginia while his old regiment marched into captivity.

Colonel Hans Christian Febiger was one of the more colorful officers. Born in Denmark, Febiger came to Massachusetts in 1772 from the island of St. Croix in the Caribbean, where he was engaged in trade. He set up his business in Boston, where he traded in lumber, horses and fish. After the Battles of Lexington and Concord, Febiger threw his support behind the colonists and joined the army as a lieutenant in Colonel Samuel Gerrish's Regiment; he was later appointed adjutant. The regiment performed poorly in the Battle of Bunker Hill, where it was called to reinforce the fort on Breed's Hill. As the regiment came under fire from the British navy, Colonel Gerrish panicked and shouted to his men to retreat or be captured. The only officer able to rally anyone was Febiger; he led a small group of the regiment to the battle and fought as part of the rear guard.[27]

Christian Febiger. *Miriam and Ira D. Wallach Division of Art, Prints and Photographs: Print Collection, New York Public Library Digital Collections.*

Following the battle at Bunker Hill, Febiger was assigned to serve as brigade major for General Benedict Arnold during the Quebec Campaign. Taken prisoner in the fighting at Quebec, Febiger was not exchanged until August 1776, when he lobbied for a commission and was made lieutenant colonel of the Eleventh Virginia Regiment.[28] He led the Eleventh Virginia Regiment at Brandywine and Germantown, after which he was transferred to the Second Virginia Regiment with the rank of colonel. Febiger was one of the best colonels in the Virginia Line at the time and was selected to command one of Anthony Wayne's light infantry regiments in the spring of 1779. The taking of Stony Point was one of the high points of his career. He claimed to be one of the first inside the fort there and took credit for personally capturing the British commander.[29] He continued to command his regiment in the light infantry until the corps was disbanded in November 1779.

Colonel Febiger remained in Philadelphia in January 1780 to command the battalion of Virginians left in that city. He was ordered to remain there with them until they were discharged in the spring. Muhlenberg had hoped to use Febiger for recruiting in Virginia, but Febiger remained in Philadelphia to gather and send supplies to the Virginia troops. He returned to Virginia in 1781 to more confusion than he could have imagined.

Colonel John Green was born in 1730 in Culpeper County, Virginia, the son of Robert Green, who came to Virginia in 1710 at the age of seventeen. Robert established a plantation called Liberty Hall, where he raised his family. Robert Green was described as nearly six feet tall, and he had seven sons (including John) who were all similarly large. Each son also took after his mother with his red hair; the family became known as the Red

Greens of Culpeper.[30] The redheaded John Green began the Revolution as a captain of riflemen in the First Virginia Regiment in 1775. He was promoted to major of the First Virginia in 1776 and marched north in August 1776. He was severely wounded in the right shoulder during an engagement near New Rochelle, New York, on October 21, 1776. Two musket balls struck him in the shoulder and passed through his body, damaging his shoulder blade. Despite his wounds, he returned to lead the First Virginia at the Battle of Trenton just over two months later. He fought in most of the battles with General Washington from Trenton to Monmouth and rose to the rank of colonel by the end of 1777. Green took command of a detachment consisting of the First and Sixth Virginia Regiments during the Siege of Fort Mifflin in November 1777.[31]

Military service had not been kind to Colonel Green. He was now fifty years old, a veteran of five years, and his old wound made it hard to move his right arm. Colonel Green was not selected to command troops to go to Charleston and went home to Culpeper County. He did not return to service until November 1780 and took command of a new battalion at Chesterfield Courthouse soon after.

Lieutenant Colonel Richard Campbell was anxious to return to service east of the Appalachian Mountains in September 1780. From the Shenandoah Valley like General Muhlenberg, Campbell was one of the original captains in Muhlenberg's Eighth Virginia in 1776 and rose to lieutenant colonel of the Thirteenth Virginia Regiment.[32] The Thirteenth Virginia (reorganized as the Ninth Virginia in September 1778) was raised mostly from the parts of Virginia that became western Pennsylvania, Maryland and West Virginia and consisted mostly of riflemen. Only five companies came from Fort Pitt to fight with Washington around Philadelphia, and Campbell was with them when they fought at Brandywine and Germantown, where he was slightly wounded.[33] After Germantown, several officers of the regiment were tried for cowardly actions during the battle, and the Thirteenth Virginia's withdrawal at that battle drew criticism for precipitating the collapse of the American left flank.[34]

Campbell marched his men to Valley Forge and expected to take part in the next campaign. The men, however, were ready to go home. It was decided that the regiment would be of better service on the frontier at Fort Pitt rather than marching with Washington. The regiment left in May 1778, marched to Fort Pitt and remained there for the remainder of its service.[35] Colonel Campbell, however, was not happy with this decision. He took part in several small campaigns from Fort Pitt and fought in skirmishes with American

Indians, but he longed to be back east fighting the British. In the spring of 1780, Campbell returned to Virginia on army business but remained to help organize the old soldiers and new recruits at Chesterfield Courthouse. While at Chesterfield, Campbell proposed that he be transferred to command troops in the Southern Army.[36] He commanded troops in eastern Virginia during the Leslie Raid in the fall of 1780, and finally, in February 1781, he received his transfer to command a new battalion of Virginians, which was destined to go fight in the South.[37]

Lieutenant Colonel Thomas Gaskins was the son of a wealthy landowner from Northumberland County. Gaskins raised a company of soldiers to serve in the Fifth Virginia Regiment in February and March 1776.[38] After serving with the Fifth Virginia during Washington's retreat across New Jersey, Gaskins was sent back to Virginia to recruit men to fill the ranks of his company. While recruiting there, Gaskins missed his chance to prove himself at Trenton and Princeton. He was successful in recruiting twenty-nine more men for his company and helped his brother-in-law Edwin Hull recruit his company for the Fifteenth Virginia.[39]

Once he rejoined his company in New Jersey, Gaskins found that nearly 29 percent of his original company had died of disease or deserted. At the Battle of Brandywine, Gaskins' company faced heavy fire toward the end of the day but reported no losses. At the Battle of Germantown, the Fifth Virginia was nearly surrounded during the retreat, but unlike the doomed Ninth Virginia, Gaskins and his men were able to fight their way out. In November 1777, Gaskins was promoted to major of the Fifth Virginia, and the following year, he was promoted to lieutenant colonel when the Third and Fifth Virginia Regiments were consolidated to create the Third Virginia Regiment under Colonel William Heth.[40]

Over the next two years, Gaskins spent part of his time with the army in New York and New Jersey and then part of the time in Virginia to assist in recruitment. He marched with the Virginia Line from New Jersey in December 1779, but when the Virginia Line was divided into the detachments to go to Charleston, Gaskins was one of the officers chosen not to go south. With no command, Gaskins returned to his home in Northumberland and entered into business. He remained at home until General Muhlenberg ordered him back into service in August 1780 to oversee the recruitment and drafting of new soldiers in his home county.

Lieutenant Colonel Samuel Hawes was one of the first company commanders in the Virginia Line. Before the Revolution began, in November 1774, Hawes served as clerk of the Caroline County Committee of Safety.[41]

He raised a company of regulars for the Second Virginia Regiment in Caroline County in the winter of 1776 and joined the regiment at Williamsburg. He continued to command his company in all the battles of the Philadelphia Campaign. The day after the Battle of Germantown, Hawes was promoted to the rank of major in the Tenth Virginia Regiment.[42] He was promoted to lieutenant colonel of the regiment in March 1778 and continued with the regiment through 1780. Hawes, however, was not present with the Virginia Brigade when it marched to Charleston and thus avoided capture. He was present with the regiment in December 1779, and it is possible he was either ordered to remain in Virginia or allowed to go home on furlough like other officers.

Regardless of the reason, Colonel Hawes avoided capture at Charleston and was one of the most senior officers left in the Virginia Line. He reported to duty at Chesterfield Courthouse in the fall of 1780 to take command of a new battalion made up mostly of new levies.

Lieutenant Colonel Thomas Posey was one of the more prominent officers of the Virginia Line toward the end of the Revolution and eventually led the last battalion formed in Virginia during the last years of the conflict. Born along the Potomac River adjacent to Washington's Mount Vernon plantation and later moved to the Shenandoah Valley, Posey had prior military experience as an officer in the Virginia forces during the Battle of Point Pleasant in 1774. He was commissioned as captain to raise a company of riflemen from Botetourt County and assigned to the Seventh Virginia Regiment.[43] He led his troops against Lord Dunmore at the Battle of Gwynn's Island and marched to join General Washington in January 1777. He served as a captain in Daniel Morgan's Rifle Regiment during the Saratoga Campaign and in the Monmouth Campaign in 1778. He took command of the Rifle Regiment after it was reduced to two companies and served for some time in upstate New York.

Oil portrait of Thomas Posey by artist John Bayless Hill (1849–1874), who based it on a miniature painted in 1795 by James Peale (1749–1831). *Public domain.*

Posey was promoted to major of the Seventh Virginia Regiment in December 1778 and was placed as a battalion commander in General Anthony Wayne's light infantry corps in the spring of 1779.

Posey claimed to have been one of the first men to enter the fort during the Battle of Stony Point. He was one of the officers detailed to recruit in Virginia in 1780 and thus missed the disasters of the South. Following Charleston, officers were ordered to disperse across the state to help gather recruits and drafted men and bring them to Chesterfield Courthouse to form the new battalions. Major Posey was stationed at Staunton, Virginia, and was in charge of gathering recruits in the Shenandoah Valley. He also briefly commanded militia in 1780 and 1781.[44]

## Company Officers of the Virginia Line

The officer corps of the Virginia Line, much like the rest of the organization, was hit hard by the disasters of 1780 and took some time to recover. In the spring of 1781, of the 244 officers who were considered part of the Virginia Continental Line, 107 were still in service in some capacity, with over half of them in service with General Greene's Southern Army.[45] Ninety-six of the officers were still prisoners at Charleston, while the remaining officers were either paroled or on furlough or could not be located.[46] This led to consistent issues with command and discipline in the Virginia Line after 1780. General Greene complained to officials that he did not have enough officers for the Virginia troops under his command and that, at times, whole companies lacked officers; many had only one officer present. Colonel Febiger complained of the same issue when he saw the condition of his old battalion just after the Siege of Yorktown in late 1781. Many junior officers were removed in February 1781, when the Virginia Line was reorganized into eight regiments and the most junior officer of each rank (from ensign to colonel) was declared a supernumerary officer and thus lacked a command. This meant the most senior officers would remain in the field with the troops.

Nathanael Greene. *Miriam and Ira D. Wallach Division of Art, Prints and Photographs: Print Collection, New York Public Library Digital Collections.*

The officer corps that was in the field, however, were made up of mostly experienced men. The vast majority of the officers had been in service for at least three years, and a handful of the original 1775 officers of the first two regiments were still in service. Captain Andrew Wallace of the Eighth Virginia originally commanded an independent company on the Virginia frontier, for the first two years of the war, and then served in the Twelfth Virginia Regiment. Captain Thomas Hord still bore a scar on his face from a British sword at the Battle of Waxhaws when he returned to the South in 1781. Some of the officers were new to the Continental Army. Lieutenant Colonel Campbell allowed his son Archibald to join the army, and Archibald was commissioned as an ensign in October 1780.[47] Colonel Green did the same and brought his son Robert and nephew Gabriel into service as ensigns around the same time.[48]

The officers did have disagreements among themselves. The subject of seniority had always been an issue within the Virginia Line, and the summer and fall of 1780 were no different. With all the Virginia regiments gone and detachments of recruits beginning to be organized into companies and battalions, debates about who was the most senior officer and thus deserved a command in the new battalions was had at Chesterfield. Lieutenant Conway Oldham of the Eighth Virginia wrote to Colonel Davies on March 22, 1781, while in camp following the battle at Guilford Courthouse, to complain about the appointment of Lieutenant Robert Jouett of the same regiment as captain-lieutenant.[49] Oldham claimed he was entitled to the appointment over Jouett, as he considered himself senior. He was pleased to be promoted to captain shortly afterward and continued to outrank Jouett.

## VETERANS OF THE VIRGINIA LINE AND VOLUNTEERS

The rank and file of the Virginia Line, while not necessarily having the same drama with seniority as the officers had, were more complicated than their commanding officers when it came to organization and motives for enlistments. In May 1780, about eighty to one hundred Continental veterans were still left in Virginia from the Virginia Line when it marched south due to lack of clothing.[50] Combined with the remains of Colonel Abraham Buford's Third Virginia Detachment, this left roughly two hundred officers and men in the Virginia Continental Line. There was hope that a new battalion could be raised to rejoin the Southern Army under General Johann de Kalb.[51] Though Buford's Battalion eventually arrived in North Carolina, it took some time for them to march. Those who did march under Buford were nowhere close to the continental quota of three thousand men from Virginia.[52] After the fall of Charleston, the new battalions of the Virginia Line were made up of veteran soldiers, new volunteers, drafted men and substitutes.

The veterans who escaped capture at Charleston and the disaster at Waxhaws formed the core of the new Virginia Battalions, particularly the battalion from Colonel Buford. Like the officers who commanded the companies formed throughout the end of the war, the enlisted men had fought in many of the major battles of the war, including Brandywine, Monmouth and Stony Point. Private James McDade had served three years in the Twelfth Virginia Regiment. Following his discharge, he reenlisted for another eighteen months in Hampshire County.[53] Sergeant Samuel Burke had served three years in the Seventh Virginia Regiment before he joined the Third Virginia Detachment and was one of the few survivors of the battle at Waxhaws.[54] Well over half of the battalion Colonel Buford led to North Carolina in August 1780 was made up of veteran soldiers. Between the spring of 1781 and the end of the war in 1783, over 1,400 Virginians enlisted for Continental service; roughly 200 of these men were veterans. Most of the veterans had served in the Virginia Line, but others had moved to the state and served in other regiments. Recruiters from Georgia were allowed to enlist men for several months in Virginia to fill their ranks. Rice Ennis was sixteen years old when he enlisted in the Third Georgia Battalion from his home county of Goochland and served three years. Four years later, Ennis was drafted for eighteen months' service in the Virginia Line.[55] John Fram also served for a year in the First Georgia Battalion before he enlisted in August 1780 under Captain John Overton.[56] The English-born Richard Turner had already served three years in the Sixth Maryland Regiment when he enlisted for the duration of the war in Lancaster County, Virginia, in December 1780.[57] Veterans also came from the Continental Line regiments from Pennsylvania, North Carolina and South Carolina, as well as the Continental dragoons, both the Virginia State and the Continental Artillery and the Virginia State Navy. There were even two recruits in 1781 who had formerly served in the British army.

Some of the new recruits enlisted voluntarily in the Virginia Line in the second half of the American Revolution, for different reasons. Some enlisted because of their political beliefs, others for the chance to earn bounty money and land in exchange for their service. Moses Rollins, a recruit from Culpeper County, later stated he had "cheerfully enlisted in the defense of my country."[58] He served three years in the Carolinas and Georgia. Some enlisted to get away from their troubles at home. Asher Crockett was sixteen years old when he ran away from his master in Hampshire County to join the Continental Army in 1776. After serving two years as a waiter to officers, he returned to Hampshire County, only to find his old master trying to reclaim him. To avoid servitude, Crockett decided to join the army. He joined as a substitute, and after that, he was rejected for his height. Colonel Hite, the county lieutenant for Hampshire County, made a deal with Crockett: Hite would accept him into service if he enlisted for three years. Crockett agreed and enlisted under the alias James Anderson. He later joined the Third Virginia Detachment in 1779, and he continued to serve in the Carolinas as well in Virginia.[59]

Tapley Lightfoot was a nineteen-year-old apprentice planter from Hanover County in 1780. After quarrelling with his master, Lightfoot ran away from his service to join the Continental Army.[60] John Redinhour used the Continental Army as his escape from his abusive father. His older brother George had enlisted for the same reason and was killed at Brandywine in 1777. After having enough of his father's treatment, John enlisted for three years at Staunton under Captain Thomas Bell in the summer of 1780. John's father tried to retrieve him from the army. Captain Bell and his officers knew of John's father's temperament and made efforts to conceal John from him. John served his three years and moved to Kentucky after the end of his service. His brother Joseph and the rest of the family assumed he was dead and believed this for thirty years, until Joseph moved to the same county as John.[61]

## Drafted Men and Substitutes

As the war dragged on, the number of veterans returning to service dwindled. As stated earlier, Colonel Buford's battalion contained many veterans in August 1780. The following battalions had fewer veterans as each one was formed, usually less than one quarter of their respective strength each. After five years of war and inflation, many Virginians were tired of the recruiting parties, and it became extremely difficult to fill the Continental quota with volunteers and veterans alone. The Virginia General Assembly decided that conscription was the best system for filling the ranks of the Virginia Line.

Throughout 1780 and '81, drafts were held in all Virginia counties east of the Shenandoah Valley. Each county was required to provide one-fifteenth of the men from its militia for Continental service. Those who were drafted were to serve for eighteen months but were allowed to hire substitutes to serve in their place. Humphrey Hill was a seventeen-year-old planter from Middlesex County when he was drafted for eighteen months of service in the Continental Army.[62] Achilis Hoskins, an eighteen-year-old from King and Queen County, was enticed by one group of men to act as their substitute for "$5,000 in old continental money."[63] Edward Greenelsh, a thirty-three-year-old Englishman, accepted a $1,000 note of tobacco (paper currency) as payment when he was marched from Shenandoah County for eighteen months' service.[64] William Dennis was twenty-five-years old when he left Northampton County on the Eastern Shore as a substitute in the fall of 1780.[65]

The story of William Higgins is one of the more interesting about a substitute. Higgins moved to Loudoun County from England before the Revolution and was a thirty-five-year-old butcher when the draft was held in the county. Higgins was bound to a gentleman named James Lewis, and Lewis placed Higgins as a substitute for another man. In his pension application, Higgins did not state if he was ever paid, but Lewis did receive one enslaved man to work for one year and two hogsheads of tobacco for supplying Higgins as a substitute.[66] Higgins had been serving for four months when he was offered land and money if he enlisted for the duration of the war. He took this offer and served for twenty months before he was sent home ill. While in the service, Higgins married, and his wife, Margaret, followed him through the service, one of the few named camp followers in the Virginia Line.

John Foster made a mistake when he enlisted as a substitute. The seventeen-year-old resident of Prince William County enlisted in April 1781 with the understanding that he had done so for eighteen months. Records, however, indicated he enlisted for three years instead. At the end of his supposed eighteen months' enlistment, Foster went to Captain Clough Shelton, his company commander in South Carolina. He requested his discharge and was informed that he had enlisted for three years. "I protested against it but in vain," Foster wrote in his pension application in 1841, and he continued to serve until he was discharged in Richmond in the summer of 1783.[67]

## Demographics of the Virginia Line, 1780–83

Beginning in June 1780, the veterans and new recruits of the Virginia Continental Line were brought to Chesterfield Courthouse, Virginia, to be formed into new battalions and sent to the Southern Army. Over the next three years, roughly 2,200 Virginians were gathered and enlisted at Chesterfield Courthouse or other recruiting stations around Virginia. Including the roughly 200 Continentals still in the field after May 1780, the strength of the Virginia Continental Line over the last three years of the Revolutionary War was roughly 2,400, though it does not appear that more than 1,300 were in the field and fit for service at any given time.[68] None of the enlisted men wrote memoirs after the end of their service, and much of what is known of their personal service has been obtained from their pension applications. Beginning in 1818, Continental veterans were able to apply for pensions from the federal government as long as they had served at least nine months. State pensions were also granted to those who were disabled after the Revolution. These pension applications provide a glimpse into their service, and some are rich with details about their officers, the battles and where they marched and camped. Size rolls were taken at several locations, such as Chesterfield Courthouse, throughout the last three years of war to account for basic information about new recruits. These records prove valuable for not only naming each man and boy who enlisted or was

Chesterfield County courthouse. *Wikimedia Commons CC BY-SA 4.0.*

drafted for Continental service but also giving their physical description (such as their height), their age and background information about them, such as their occupation, birthplace, residence and previous service, if applicable.

Over the last three years of war, the average age of a soldier in the Virginia Continental Line was twenty-four years old. The youngest was twelve-year-old Elijah Coplin of Prince George County, who was measured shortly after enlisting at the Cumberland Old Courthouse station on July 28, 1782, where he enlisted for duration of the war.[69] The oldest was sixty-five-year-old Edward White, who was a distiller from Botetourt County.[70] He enlisted for two years on April 29, 1782, and was measured at the Albemarle Old Courthouse station.

The size rolls also have information on the birthplaces of the soldiers. Of the 2,103 men and boys who had identifiable birthplaces, approximately 80 percent were born within the original Thirteen Colonies. The vast majority were born in Virginia, with Maryland and Pennsylvania close behind. Roughly 20 percent of the recruits (427) were foreign-born. A plurality of foreign-born recruits (192, or 45 percent) hailed from England; about one-third were born in Ireland. The remaining foreign-born recruits hailed from nine other countries or regions. John Smith, who was drafted for three years in Orange County in March 1781, was born in Jamaica.[71] The Italian-born John Hallica enlisted for eighteen months from Isle of Wight County, where he worked as a tailor, in September 1780.[72] John Temm was the only known man in the Virginia Line after 1780 to be born in Sweden; he enlisted as a substitute in Culpeper County in March 1781 at the age of forty-five.[73]

The occupations listed in the size rolls were reflective of the agricultural background of Virginians. The occupations of 1,814 of the men can be identified, and roughly 63 percent of them were listed as planters or farmers. Shoemaker (28 percent), carpenter (21 percent) and tailor (18 percent) made up the next three most popular occupations. Over fifty pre-service occupations were also listed between 1780 and 1783. The Scottish-born John Alexander Still left his classroom in Hanover County, where he was a schoolmaster, to serve for eighteen months in September 1780.[74] Twenty-five-year-old John Ripley was a ship's carpenter when he enlisted as a substitute in Gloucester County in August 1780.[75]

The Fourth Virginia Convention had stated in the December 1775 recruiting law, "No recruiting officer shall be allowed to enlist into the service any servant whatsoever, except apprentices bound under the laws of this colony, nor any such apprentices unless the consent of his master be first had in writing."[76] Enslaved Africans were included in this law. By

1775, roughly 40 percent of Virginia's population was enslaved. Though the December 1775 recruiting act did not allow for enslaved men to be enlisted, free men of color were allowed to enlist by the fall of 1776. Some masters in Virginia also sent enslaved men as substitutes when the state government passed draft laws in the latter half of the American Revolution. A Hessian officer remarked in December 1777 that in the Continental Army, "the negro can take the field in his master's place; hence you never see a regiment in which there are not a lot of negroes."[77] In August 1778, it was reported that Black soldiers made up roughly 4 percent of the rank and file of all Virginia regiments.[78]

According to the size rolls from different stations between 1780 and 1783, 142 men of color enlisted in the Virginia Continental Line, roughly 6 percent of all recruits raised during this period. The average age of Black recruits was thirty-one, while the average age of all recruits was twenty-four. Analysis of the eighty-nine men of color who were enlisted after 1781 (listed in the size rolls as "black," "yellow," "brown" and "mulatto") shows that just over half of these recruits were enlisted as substitutes. The same sample shows that forty-six of the eighty-nine were enlisted for eighteen months, while thirty-five were enlisted for the duration of the war, five for three years, one for two years and one for one year. Joshua Payne, a nineteen-year-old Black farmer from King George County, had already served two years in the Virginia State Navy when he enlisted as a substitute in April 1781.[79] Four recruits are also listed as "Indian" in the size roll of recruits from 1781 to 1783. James Morton, for example, was a Native American who was born in Massachusetts and worked as a sailor. He enlisted as a substitute at the age of twenty in March 1781 when he was living in Loudoun County.[80]

Overall, the Virginia Continental Line after 1780 shows the diversity of Virginia through the occupations, birthplaces and races of recruits. The overall average age of twenty-four compared to the overall average age of Continental veterans throughout the states, twenty-one, demonstrates the fact that many young recruits had already been enlisted in the Virginia Line before 1780. The presence of drafted men and substitutes also demonstrates the weariness of Virginians and their aversion to Continental service. In the next chapter, the recruiting laws of Virginia and the change in attitude to service after 1780 are explored.

Chapter 2

# METHODS OF FILLING THE RANKS OF THE VIRGINIA LINE

Through the last three years of the American Revolution, officers and state officials had to determine how best to fill the ranks of the Virginia Continental Line. Motives for and methods of recruiting had changed since the first regiments were formed in the fall of 1775. Inflation led to a rise in the bounties offered for Continental service. The lack of volunteers further necessitated conscription to meet quotas. Militia delinquents and state soldiers were transferred to Continental service to provide short-term relief to the strength of the battalion raised throughout the late war years. The officers of the Virginia Continental Line tried to reorganize the regiments that existed before May 1780 but found it difficult with the arrival of new recruits and the changes of the rank and file between continental recruits, state soldiers and drafted men.

## Recruiting Laws, Drafts and Substitutions, 1777–81

After the initial rush to arms in Virginia in 1775 and 1776, Continental recruiters found it difficult to enlist new recruits. Captain James Monroe, the future fifth president of the United States, was sent to Virginia in the spring of 1777 to recruit a company for Colonel Thurston's Additional Continental Regiment. Over the spring and summer of 1777, the young Monroe was able to recruit only fifteen men. Joseph Jones, one of Virginia's delegates to the Continental Congress and Monroe's uncle, regretted in a letter to General Washington that "some men have indeed been raised but by methods I could not recommend" and was sorry his nephew may have been one of the officers who used such ambiguous methods to which Jones doesn't specify.[81] Monroe was one of many officers who faced such a challenge in recruiting. Inflation, competition with state troops and the allure of remaining at home and only serving in the militia all kept Virginians from enlisting in Continental service. The Continental bounty of twenty dollars was not seen as enough to convince men to serve. General Washington wrote to Virginia Governor Patrick Henry in November 1777 that the Continental bounty was "fruitless" and the sums paid for militia substitutes were so large that any men who might consider Continental service preferred militia service, where "neither duty or discipline" were as severe.[82] The Virginia General Assembly had approved a limited draft in 1777 and 1779, and in the summer of 1780, it approved a full draft.

In May 1780, the Virginia General Assembly passed two new laws. The first, "an act to embody militia for the relief of South Carolina, and for other purposes," was meant to raise 2,500 militiamen to serve as infantry and another fifty to serve as a troop of cavalry "in legal rotation" with other militia cavalry companies in the Southern Army for three months, beginning from when they joined the army.[83] The second, "an act for speedily recruiting the quota of this state for the continental army," called for 3,000 men to be raised to complete the state's continental quota; these men were to serve until December 31, 1781.[84] The militia responded faster than the Continental troops from Virginia. The fact that their men were not captured at Charleston made it possible for them to mobilize quickly and report for duty, no matter how unreliable they proved to be later in the year.

Each county was ordered to furnish one-fifteenth of its militia thirty days after receiving information about the 1780 Recruiting Act and dividing its militia into "divisions" of fifteen men each.[85] Each division of the county militia, sometimes referred to as "classes," would then send one man, and if any county failed to fill its quota within thirty days of laying off, or creating, the divisions, then the county would enact a draft. The draft was to include all freemen between eighteen and fifty, except for those who marched with the militia to South Carolina. Quakers or Mennonites could be excused as well, but they were expected to provide a substitute at the expense of their society. If they failed to provide a substitute, the county sheriff was authorized to levy payments or gather goods to make up for the payment for the substitute.[86] All those who were drafted would serve for eighteen months. Drafted men could also provide a substitute to serve in their place. Each division was also allowed to collect funds in order to hire a man to serve eighteen months in the Virginia Line.[87] The usual bounties were granted to all men who joined the Virginia Line, whether they were drafted or volunteered. In addition to this law, any delinquents from the militia, if found guilty, were ordered to serve six to eight months in the Continental Army.

A similar law was passed by the Virginia General Assembly in October 1780 after the May 1780 Recruiting Act failed to gather enough men to fill the quota; only eight hundred men of the three thousand called for in May 1780 reported. The new act, "an act for recruiting this state's quota of troops to serve in the continental army," gave each county another quota equal to one-fifteenth of its militia and fifty days from dividing the militia into groups called divisions to fill its quota.[88] The bounties for Continental service were increased. Each recruit who enlisted for the duration of the war was to receive $12,000, while those who enlisted for three years were entitled to $8,000. The effects of inflation over five years of war are evident in this recruiting tactic, as well as the desperation of the state government to fill the ranks. All men who were already enlisted and anyone who enlisted for duration of the war before April 1, 1781, were entitled to choose either a "healthy" slave between ten and thirty years old or sixty pounds in gold or silver. In addition, they were entitled to three hundred acres of land in lieu of all such bounties given by any former laws.[89] Recruiters were instructed to enlist men who were prisoners of war, deserters from the British army or engaged to serve for longer than eight months.[90] Drafted men were allowed a bounty of $4,000. In addition, any militiamen who ran away during the Battle of Camden in August 1780 were sentenced to serve eight months in the Continental Army and were dubbed Eight Months' Men.[91]

## Draft Resistance

General Peter Muhlenberg thought the citizens of Virginia would agree with the draft. A draft for 2,500 militiamen to be sent to the South at the same time was underway, and the Virginia General Assembly was considering another draft of 5,000 men for militia service. Muhlenberg thought the mass drafting of militia might convince Virginians that the state needed a regular force instead of relying on militia.[92] Muhlenberg's opinion was inaccurate, and there was resistance in several counties in Virginia. In Augusta County, the draft had not taken place by May 1781. Major Thomas Posey, the recruiting officer at Staunton, complained to Colonel William Davies that he had collected only twenty-one men, whom he described as "deserters and others."[93] Major Posey observed that the people of Augusta and Rockbridge Counties were against the draft and that in both counties, mobs had arrived at the courthouse, seized the militia papers and destroyed them, believing there could be no draft if the militia rolls did not exist. Posey went on to suggest to Colonel Davies that only the hanging of a few of these men to set an example would stop this behavior. Other counties experienced similar reactions to the draft, but Northumberland and Accomack Counties had the most notable reactions within Virginia.

Northumberland County was prepared to resist the draft in September 1780 by any means necessary. The county, situated on the end of the Northern Neck, was subjected to loyalist privateers throughout the war, further dividing loyalties. Thomas Gaskins Sr., the county lieutenant and father of Lieutenant Colonel Thomas Gaskins Jr., expected some trouble in implementing the draft in Northumberland. He asked his captains to gather some men to help suppress any riotous activity but found that very few of the militia were willing to come out, as they were also against the draft.[94] On September 15, 1780, Colonel Gaskins Sr., his son and other militia officers gathered at the courthouse at Heathsville. Present was Captain Edwin Hull, who had been declared a supernumerary officer from the Fifteenth Virginia in September 1778 and was acting as a recruiting officer in Northumberland.[95] Around that time, a crowd of 150 men gathered outside the courthouse with clubs and arms, intending to prevent the draft.[96]

Captain Hull and Lieutenant George Eskridge (another supernumerary officer from the former Fifteenth Virginia) were sent with a flag of truce to talk to the crowd, while Gaskins and some volunteers observed. Hull and Eskridge led the crowd to the green, where a small detail of volunteers stood. One of the rioters passed by Hull with a firelock on his shoulder. Hull, who carried a musket himself, called on the man to lay down his arms, to which the man replied, "You ground *your* firearm."[97] The two men took aim and fired on each other at the same time. Both were mortally wounded. More shots were fired from both sides. Several men were wounded, including Gaskins Jr. After that, Gaskins Sr. and a company of thirty-two men, mostly officers, quelled the rest of the rioters and subdued "almost the whole county."[98] Fifty of the rioters were sentenced by court martial to serve for the duration of the war in the Virginia Line, though nine of their sentences were reduced to just eighteen months. It was also reported that some of the rioters had "gone over to the enemy" to avoid service.[99]

Accomack County protested against the draft, and the protest was close to the proportions of the Northumberland draft riot. Accomack, one of the two counties that compose the Eastern Shore of Virginia, was separated from the rest of Virginia and was one of the most exposed places in the state. Throughout the Revolution, the coastline of Accomack was subject to raids by British forces and Loyalist privateers. Accomack also had one of the largest militias in the state, with 1,200 individuals between eighteen and fifty years old on the militia rolls in September 1780.[100] Though the Chesterfield 1780 size roll does not show any recruits being sized (measured) from Accomack County, a number of recruits from Accomack and Northampton Counties were brought to the Southern Army by Captain Philip Sansum. It is not clear if Accomack met its quota of eighty.[101] The draft quota was decreased to seventy-four in 1781, but a tax increase in March 1781 coupled with another draft infuriated the populace of Accomack. That same month, the men of Northampton County protested the draft, and this inspired the men of Accomack.

The county lieutenant of Accomack, Colonel George Corbin, appointed April 23 as the date the new draft would go into effect. On that day, 150 to 200 men "armed with clubs" assembled at the courthouse to oppose the draft.[102] Colonel Corbin tried to sooth the protesters, but his arguments did not appeal to them. One of the divisions produced a recruit, but before the officers marked any names off the list of the militia, one of the protestors came into the courthouse and took the list to the cheers of the mob, which had followed him into the courthouse. Corbin and other gentlemen in the courthouse decided it was impossible to continue the draft and postponed it until April 26. On the second attempt, a crowd of 200 men armed with guns, swords and clubs took over the courthouse.[103] After Corbin recovered control of the county, over twenty men were sentenced by court martial to Continental service.[104] Corbin believed the people were upset over not only the taxes and the draft but also the constant raids along the coast and the fact that their militia had been in the field constantly for nearly three years.[105]

Other counties refused to draft because of the number of their militia in the field throughout 1780 and 1781. In February 1781, Powhatan County decided to lay the county off into divisions for the draft but not to implement the draft until all its men returned from General Greene's Army.[106] The county had already sent at least a quarter of its militia into the field for seven of the past eight months. Colonel Littleberry Mosby Sr., the county lieutenant for Powhatan, tried to put the draft into action again in April 1781, only for the militia to again be called out for the British advance on

Petersburg a few days later, forcing him to again postpone the draft.[107] Other counties followed suit, and they were at times legally protected. Under both the May and October 1780 recruiting laws, counties could postpone the draft if they had any portion of their militia in the field. This was consistently an issue as British forces appeared in the state throughout 1780 and 1781. Militia was constantly kept in the field to repel the invaders in addition to the militia that was sent to the Southern Army.

## Transfer of Virginia State Troops

In the spring of 1777, three new regiments were raised for state service. In comparison to the Virginia Continental Line, the Virginia State Line was intended to serve only within the borders of Virginia unless authorized by the governor or the General Assembly. Casualties and the loss of the Ninth Virginia Regiment resulted in the state regiments, reduced to two regiments in 1778, being transferred to Continental service. The First and Second Virginia State Regiments spent the entirety of their service in Washington's Army under the command of General Muhlenberg and experienced battle alongside their Continental comrades at Monmouth, Stony Point, Paulus Hook and in other skirmishes in the northern states. The two state regiments marched from their camp at Morristown, New Jersey, on December 9, 1779, just before the Virginia Continental regiments did, and arrived in Virginia in early January 1780.[108] The First and Second State Regiments were back in state service, but they required reorganization.

The majority of the men of the two regiments had enlisted for three years starting in the spring of 1777. After May 1780, over three-quarters of the men of the two regiments would no longer be in service and return home. The men lacked pay, like the Continental regiments, and many did not intend to reenlist. In the spring of 1779, only 150 men from the two regiments had reenlisted for the duration of the war in exchange for furloughs in the winter.[109] The two regiments were marched to Alexandria, Virginia, where the enlisted men were granted furloughs. The furloughs began once they arrived in January 1780, and the men were ordered to report to Williamsburg or Fredericksburg by May 1, 1780.[110] Those who gathered at Fredericksburg were marched to Williamsburg to receive their final pay and be discharged—or, as the officers hoped, with renewed energy after resting at home, reenlist for another three years or duration of the war.

General George Washington. *Miriam and Ira D. Wallach Division of Art, Prints and Photographs: Print Collection, New York Public Library Digital Collections.*

The State of Virginia also lacked the funds to reenlist the men in the state regiments. This was another reason to furlough the men, with hopes that money could be raised by April 1780 to pay them and entice them to reenlist. The officers hoped that by the May 1 deadline for men to report to Williamsburg, there would be enough money, and the two regiments would be ready for service again.[111] The state regiments were also ordered to report to Charleston with the rest of the Virginia Line, but difficulties kept them from marching toward the South.[112] Just before the men were furloughed, the arms of the First and Second State Regiments were taken, and thus the men were unarmed when they arrived at Williamsburg. The two regiments numbered around 230 officers and men, including men enlisted for the duration of the war and for three years and new recruits.[113] These men were marched to Petersburg in early June to receive new muskets.

The two regiments acted as one, with Colonel George Gibson of the First Virginia State Regiment taking overall command. The thirty-three-year-old Gibson had lived in the mountains of present-day Pennsylvania and raised a company of riflemen for the First Virginia Regiment in 1775. He served less than a year and went back into the mountains, where he led a secret mission to bring ten thousand pounds of gunpowder from Spanish-held Louisiana to Virginia.[114] He became the colonel of the First Virginia State Regiment in the summer of 1777 and had led the regiment for most of its existence. Now he commanded what remained of the two regiments, hoping their ranks would grow in the future. Though the two regiments were ordered back to state service, they did not remain in it for long. In July 1780, Governor Jefferson made it clear to Colonel Gibson that as many of his soldiers who could be made ready were ordered to join the Southern Army.[115] Gibson and his men were officially transferred to Continental service by order of Governor Jefferson the following month.[116]

Colonel Gibson's men were not the only Virginia State Line units sent to the South in Continental service. In addition to the Virginia Continental Line, a detachment of Virginia State Troops was organized to go to Charleston. The Virginia State Artillery, two troops from Major John Nelson's State Cavalry and volunteers from the Virginia State Garrison Regiment made up a detachment led by Lieutenant Colonel Charles Porterfield. The officers and the men were considered part of the Continental establishment for six months, beginning in April 1780. Porterfield was one of the original members of Daniel Morgan's riflemen in 1775 who were captured at Quebec, and he later became a captain in the Eleventh Virginia Regiment.[117] He was allegedly the first to fire a shot and hit a British soldier at the Battle of Brandywine and was later promoted to major.[118] In the spring of 1779, Porterfield left the Continental establishment to become the major of the Virginia State Garrison Regiment that was organized the previous year.[119] Like the First and Second State Regiments, the State Garrison Regiment was formed with an understanding that the men were meant for service only within Virginia.

First and Second Virginia Continental Regiments, circa 1781. *Courtesy of Don Troiani.*

In all, 106 officers and men from the State Garrison Regiment volunteered for service in the South because they were to be considered part of the Virginia Continental Line for six months, which meant they received both Continental and state pay for those six months.[120]

Regardless of whether the men who joined after 1780 were volunteers, were drafted for military service, enlisted for adventure, money or personal reasons or were state soldiers who were being asked to do more than what was expected of them—they all filled the ranks of the Virginia Continental Line through the late war years. All the officers and men who served in the Virginia Continental Line after the fall of Charleston were destined to do their part to attempt to control the South. In battalions that this book will discuss, they played an important role in the struggle of the southern states and the eventual victory that created a nation.

## Chapter 3

# REORGANIZATION

## Organization of the Recruiting Service

General Muhlenberg came to Virginia with new instructions. While the rest of the Virginia Line, with all the men he had commanded over the past four years, marched to Charleston and eventual disaster, Muhlenberg reported to Virginia away from what was considered the front lines. The Continental Congress ordered Muhlenberg to await orders from General Washington there and, while in Virginia, to superintend and collect all the recruits in the state for Continental service.[121] Washington wrote to Muhlenberg that "every reasonable exertion" to get recruits would depend on Muhlenberg.[122] In a letter dated April 20, 1780, Washington laid out for Muhlenberg how he wanted to organize the recruits and begin funneling reinforcements to the South.

The first subject that Washington discussed with Muhlenberg was the place of general rendezvous. General Scott had chosen Petersburg as the general rendezvous for all recruits to be gathered the year before. Washington complained, based on Scott's letters, that Petersburg was an unhealthy location for recruits to be gathered and had "proved to be the grave of too many."[123] Washington next suggested that Muhlenberg chose a field officer to superintend the recruiting service while Muhlenberg himself remained in total control of all Virginia forces. Washington proposed that as new recruits and drafted men were brought into camp, they would be immediately formed into companies of at least fifty men and, once disciplined, sent south

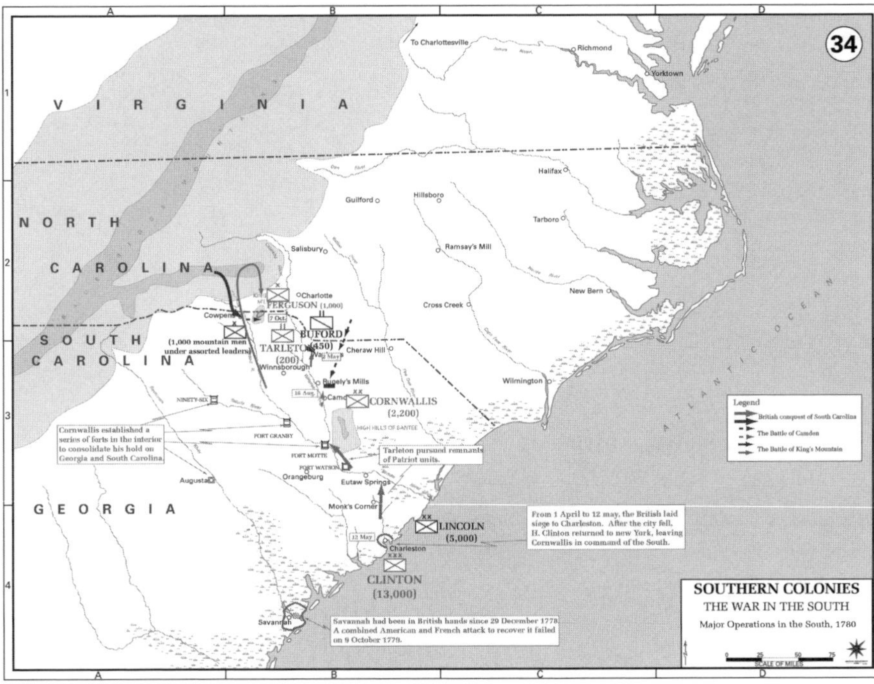


Map of the Southern Theater and military movements. *Courtesy of the United States Military Academy Department of History.*

as soon as possible. When they had collected over 150 men, a field officer should take command and send them south. Special attention was also to be given to collecting furloughed soldiers and deserters. Finally, Washington asked Muhlenberg to keep him constantly updated on the conditions of the recruiting service in Virginia. All this was planned before the capture of Charleston and was not planned for Muhlenberg to completely rebuild the Virginia Continental Line.

Muhlenberg immediately went to Williamsburg in April to meet with Governor Thomas Jefferson, only to find Jefferson absent, at his home in Albemarle County, and the seat of the state government being moved to Richmond. He rode to the new capital of Virginia and met Jefferson there. On arrival, Muhlenberg learned from Jefferson that he should expect little from the draft and that there was no money in the treasury to help with recruiting.[124] Muhlenberg followed Washington's instructions to pick a central location to gather men and proposed a new general rendezvous for the recruits. He chose Rocky Ridge, which was also known as Manchester, located along the James River and directly across from the town of Richmond.

The Battle of the Waxhaws, May 29, 1780. *Miriam and Ira D. Wallach Division of Art, Prints and Photographs: Print Collection, New York Public Library Digital Collections.*

WS, MAY 29TH, 1780.

He also proposed that Fredericksburg and Winchester be used as rendezvous for smaller groups of recruits.[125] Muhlenberg proposed that officers of the Virginia Continental Line who were off duty appoint districts within their counties to gather recruits. Jefferson approved most of these proposals but disagreed with the idea of Rocky Ridge as the general rendezvous for Continental recruits. He claimed it was unhealthy and too near Richmond and proposed Chesterfield Courthouse as the new site.[126]

The village of Chesterfield Courthouse was located roughly eleven miles south of Richmond. It was further inland from the James River, away from the unhealthy encampment of Petersburg and far enough from Richmond that the possible spread of disease would not infect the capital—but also a convenient location from which to send troops to North Carolina. After viewing the site in late May, General Muhlenberg set himself to establish the new recruiting system. Fredericksburg and Winchester were selected as locations to gather recruits before they marched to Chesterfield, as his original plan dictated. He intended to place Colonel Christian Febiger in command of the recruiting station at Fredericksburg, and Colonel John Green was placed in command of the recruiting station at Winchester.[127] By late May, Muhlenberg had gathered 50 recruits to be sent toward Charleston to join the Virginia troops there. By mid-June, Muhlenberg had gathered 109 men at Chesterfield, 28 at Richmond and 20 at Fredericksburg.[128] The new recruitment system held some promise, as it was structured for smaller detachments of recruits and intended only to replace the empty ranks of existing regiments, but it was not until early June that Muhlenberg learned of the surrender at Charleston. He had hopes of reinforcing Colonel Buford in South Carolina with all available troops, but only days after learning of the defeat at Charleston, Muhlenberg learned of the disaster at Waxhaws.[129]

The new recruiting law and the lack of existing regiments after Charleston and Waxhaws necessitated a change. Though Chesterfield Courthouse remained the general rendezvous site for Virginia recruits, Muhlenberg believed the smaller stations at Fredericksburg and Winchester would not be able to handle the number of recruits entering service. The Virginia General Assembly agreed and began the process of dividing up the counties of Virginia into several districts in order to gather recruits from the different regions.[130] Muhlenberg planned to organize the new recruits into new battalions. He planned on reorganizing six regiments of the Virginia Line: the Second, Sixth, Seventh, Ninth and Eleventh Virginia Regiments. The colonels of those regiments before Charleston would assume command of these reorganized regiments. The colonels were Christian Febiger of the

Second Virginia, John Green of the Sixth Virginia, Daniel Morgan of the Seventh Virginia, John Gibson of the Ninth Virginia and Abraham Buford of the Eleventh Virginia.[131] Muhlenberg was later instructed to fill each regiment to 504 enlisted men before it was sent into the field, beginning with Febiger's Second Virginia.[132] Washington stressed to Muhlenberg and other officers the importance of the discipline of the men, as success in the South relied on "the discipline and the bravery of the Troops."[133]

## Formation of Colonel Buford's Battalion

The first fifty recruits gathered at Chesterfield Courthouse were sent to the South by June 1780. Muhlenberg returned from a tour of the Winchester recruiting station to meet more recruits and begin organizing them into units. He was joined by Colonel Buford and the survivors of Waxhaws. Following the disaster of Waxhaws, Colonel Buford was able to rally roughly one hundred officers and men in North Carolina from his shattered command. He joined the forces of General Johann de Kalb at Hillsborough, North Carolina, by June 20, 1780. Buford proposed to take his men back to Virginia to refit with arms and clothing, as well as bolster his strength with Muhlenberg's recruits. General de Kalb was reluctant to send Buford back to Virginia, but without arms and proper clothing for Buford, he allowed Buford to return to Virginia, as Buford promised to return "in a fortnight."[134] Some of Buford's men, however, remained with the Southern Army. Private Asher Crockett (the servant from Hampshire County fighting under the name James Anderson) joined with Lieutenant Colonel Porterfield's Virginia State Detachment and fought at the Battle of Camden in August.[135]

Colonel Buford and his men first marched to Petersburg to find everything in confusion. Buford's field strength was augmented by detachments of Continentals that he had left behind in the spring. Buford found that the arms he had hoped for were now absent; most of the muskets had been sent south to help the North Carolina and Virginia militia that had taken the field. The only good news for Buford was that his battalion would receive preference for clothing.[136] The men received new hunting shirts and breeches, with the promise of coats later in the year.[137]

Major General Horatio Gates assumed command of the Southern Army following the fall of Charleston in the summer of 1780. General Gates was desperate to have more troops, so he ordered Colonel Buford's battalion as well as the remnants of the First and Second Virginia State Regiments

Slaughter of Colonel Beaufort's regiment at Waxhaws. *Miriam and Ira D. Wallach Division of Art, Prints and Photographs: Print Collection, New York Public Library Digital Collections.*

to join the Southern Army in North Carolina as early as possible.[138] Gates wrongly assumed they were already uniformed and armed.[139] On August 1, 1780, Muhlenberg reported that he had collected five companies of sixty "old soldiers" each and placed them under Colonel Buford. The battalion was most likely reorganized, as by late August, Muhlenberg described the battalion as 302 "old soldiers—recruits—& deserters."[140] Buford's Battalion was joined by two companies of the First Virginia State Regiment, led by Captains Thomas W. Ewell and Windsor Brown. These two companies consisted of mostly three-year veterans. The average soldier in Buford's Battalion had at least two years of experience. In addition to all the officers having been in service for at least three years, three-quarters of the known sergeants of Buford's Battalion were veterans. Including the state soldiers, roughly two-thirds of the men in the battalion were veteran soldiers.

Colonel Buford finally marched his battalion out of Chesterfield Courthouse on August 24, 1780. New muskets were issued to the entire battalion.[141] The First and Second Virginia State Regiments, in their entirety, were also ordered to march with Buford, but the officers and men refused until they were paid, meaning the two companies of Ewell and Brown were the only state companies to march south. Knapsacks and blankets were the last supplies to arrive for Buford. The battalion, now uniformed and "well armed," as remarked by North Carolina Judge John Williams, took roughly two weeks to march into the American camp at Hillsborough, North Carolina. Only five men deserted along the march, while two were discharged at the expiration of their time. Men being detached for other duties and sick men reduced the strength of Buford's Battalion to 247. These troops arrived to find a shattered force, as the Southern Army had been defeated at the Battle of Camden in August.

Another detachment of three hundred Virginia Continentals from Chesterfield Courthouse led by Lieutenant Colonel John Webb arrived later, in September 1780, and it is unclear how long Colonel Webb remained in the South. These men were all placed under Colonel Buford's command. Other recruits did not report to Chesterfield Courthouse and were marched straight to Hillsborough, North Carolina, to join the Southern Army. Twenty-two-year-old Andrew Keyser of Shenandoah County was marched with his comrade Edward Greenelsh under Lieutenant Philip Huffman directly to North Carolina and joined Colonel Buford in the fall of 1780.[142] Captain Thomas Bell marched his entire company from Staunton, Virginia, to join the Southern Army.[143] Lieutenant Conway Oldham marched his company of recruits from Winchester, Virginia, to Hillsborough.[144] Gates disapproved of troops coming directly to his camp. He was horribly surprised when Colonel Buford's Battalion marched into camp at Hillsborough without any tents.[145] Supplies for the Southern Army, especially following the defeat at Camden in August, were low, and the arrival of new recruits only stretched those supplies further. Gates wrote to Governor Jefferson on October 6, 1780, after the arrival of recruits from Botetourt County:

> *Forty of your 18 Months Men from Bottetourt County Arrived in this Camp Yesterday, they are intirely equipped, and unprovided, with every thing that is necessary for the Service they are intended to perform, and for the Term they are engaged to serve. I must beg Sir this may be Seriously consider'd by the Executive, whom I must request, will not send any Men into the Field, or even to this Camp, that are not sufficiently Clad, well furnish'd with Shoes, Blankets, and every necessary for immediate Service, as I have not a Single Article here to Supply them with.*[146]

By October 1780, however, General Gates did receive tent cloth and had it made into tents for the men. After he was marched to join Colonel Buford's Battalion, Private Moses Rollins said, he went through the whole winter without a blanket and did not receive any new clothing until just before the Battle of Guilford Courthouse.[147] Governor Jefferson admitted to Gates that there was little chance of clothing being issued to the men and so the next battalion of recruits would be marched "cloathed as militia."[148] With the addition of Colonel Buford's Battalion, the Southern Army consisted of roughly 1,500 soldiers by September 20, 1780. The next day, Gates planned to march from Hillsborough toward Charlotte, with the intention of launching another campaign against the British.[149] The march was paused, however, to allow tents to be finished. In addition, Earl Charles Cornwallis, commander of British forces in the Southern Theater, had marched his army in the direction of Charlotte. Gates sent his new light infantry corps to the Yadkin River to watch the British and determine whether they planned to advance.

Lieutenant Colonel Charles Porterfield of Virginia had commanded Gates' light infantry at the Battle of Camden. Porterfield was mortally wounded in the battle, and his troops were trampled, much like the rest of the units at Camden. Most of the militia from Virginia and North Carolina had deserted from Gates' Army, and what remained of his light infantry corps (which had nearly three hundred officers and men at the Battle of Camden)

*Battle of Camden; Death of de Kalb*. Engraving from a painting by Alonzo Chappel. *National Archives.*

consisted of roughly fifty Virginia state soldiers led by a captain. The light infantry was reorganized into a new corps led by Colonel Daniel Morgan. Morgan joined the Southern Army in late September 1780 and organized a new corps with three companies from the Maryland Line, a company of Delaware Continentals and a company of Virginia Continentals. Captain Peter Bryan Bruin came with Colonel Morgan and, as a friend of Morgan and an experienced officer of six years, was appointed commander of the Virginia company. Bruin then went through the ranks of Colonel Buford's Battalion to pick men for the light infantry. Based on surviving records, over two-thirds of the men selected for the light infantry were veterans, and nearly one-third of those were survivors of the Waxhaws Massacre. Being a native of Frederick County, like Morgan, Bruin also appears to have favored men who were recruited from the Shenandoah Valley region or counties that bordered the Blue Ridge Mountains. Captain Bruin, however, was recalled to Virginia in November, and the command was passed to Captain Andrew Wallace, another veteran officer from Augusta County. Until early January 1781, Colonel Buford's Battalion and Captain Wallace's light infantry company were the only Virginia Continental Line units present with the Southern Army.

## Leslie's Raid

The remainder of recruits in 1780 were gathered around Chesterfield Courthouse from across the state. Some had farther to march than others. William Dennis of Northampton County was marched to meet Captain Philip Sansum with other recruits from the Eastern Shore before he was taken across the Chesapeake Bay by boat and then marched to Chesterfield.[150] By the end of November 1780, over one thousand soldiers had been gathered at Chesterfield Courthouse. Log huts were built for housing for the men, and a hospital was erected for the sick. Once the recruits began to arrive, they were assigned to companies under Continental and state officers. Though there were enough recruits to begin the process of forming battalions, the men were not prepared materially to go into the field. General Muhlenberg wrote to General Gates on October 12 that he and Colonel William Davies had tried hard to get proper equipment. "We have not been able to procure such articles as are necessary for the troops on their march," Muhlenberg explained in his letter. Blankets, especially, were "totally out of the question."[151] It was not long, though, before the Chesterfield recruits were ordered to take the field.

*Lord Cornwallis*, by John Fielding, 1786. *Library of Congress.*

British ships entered the mouth of the James River on October 20, 1780. The British fleet carried 2,200 British and Hessian soldiers led by General Alexander Leslie.[152] The overall goal of the raid was to disturb supplies heading south and divert troops away from joining General Gates, while General Earl Cornwallis led his British army from South Carolina into North Carolina. Governor Jefferson appointed General Muhlenberg to take command of all state forces to fend off Leslie's force, which had landed at Portsmouth. The Chesterfield recruits were used as the nucleus of Muhlenberg's new army. Roughly 800 men were armed and fit enough to take the field, and on October 25, Muhlenberg marched them toward Portsmouth. General George Weedon came into service from his furlough and was left in Richmond to gather militia to join Muhlenberg in the field later. Muhlenberg ordered the company officers to make good use of every opportunity to instruct the men in the drill and military discipline while on picket or other duties.[153] By November 2, the Virginia Continentals had pursued British troops to within fifteen miles of Portsmouth, but without heavy artillery or proper entrenching tools, Muhlenberg could do nothing but monitor Leslie's force. While encamped in Isle of Wight County, Muhlenberg divided the Virginia Continentals into two battalions, one led by Lieutenant Colonel Thomas Gaskins and the other by Lieutenant Colonel Samuel Hawes.

Once he received more reinforcements, Muhlenberg drove in the pickets of the enemy and confined the British in Portsmouth, but he felt he was not ready to attack the port. Once outside of Portsmouth, Muhlenberg divided his force into two brigades. The first brigade was commanded by General Weedon and consisted of Gaskins' Continental Battalion, the First Virginia State Regiment, the State Garrison Regiment and Colonel Alexander Spotswood's militia regiment. The second brigade was led by General Thomas Nelson Jr. and consisted of Hawes' Continental Battalion, the Second Virginia State Regiment, Colonel James Monroe's Militia Regiment,

Colonel Josiah Parker's Militia Regiment and another detachment of militia led by Colonel Joseph Jones. Colonel Charles Harrison brought in his men of the First Continental Artillery (all light artillery pieces), and Lieutenant Colonel Richard Campbell of the Ninth Virginia commanded the light infantry.[154] Muhlenberg had only light artillery pieces and felt they were not strong enough to attack the earthworks that protected Portsmouth. Occasional skirmishing is all that took place between the two sides before General Leslie left by ship with his troops on November 25.

## General Greene Comes South and Colonel Green's Battalion Is Formed

After disbanding the militia at Petersburg, the Virginia Continental and state troops returned to Chesterfield Courthouse to find two new commanders. Major General Nathanael Greene had been appointed to command the Southern Department in place of General Gates, and Major General Baron de Steuben followed Greene as his second-in-command.[155] Greene was raised a Quaker in Rhode Island, but despite

General Greene's headquarters. *Miriam and Ira D. Wallach Division of Art, Prints and Photographs: Print Collection, New York Public Library Digital Collections.*

his religious background, he volunteered with the Rhode Island Militia in 1774 and led Rhode Island troops around Boston in 1775. Greene quickly became one of Washington's most trusted generals and was appointed the quartermaster general for Washington's Army in 1778. His organizational skills and experience leading combat troops would serve him well in the South.

Friedrich Wilhelm Ludolf Gerhard Augustin Louis von Steuben was an experienced Prussian officer who arrived in America in 1778 and was credited with instilling discipline and restructuring Washington's Army at Valley Forge. The "Drillmaster of Valley Forge" was appointed inspector general with the rank of major general and wrote the new manual for the Continental Army. Greene found the military situation in Virginia in the "greatest state of confusion imaginable."[156] Greene also reported that over two thousand Virginians had volunteered or had been drafted for Continental service, but mass desertion and disease weakened the strength of the Virginia Continental Line to roughly eight hundred.[157] General Steuben was ordered to remain in Virginia to reorganize and train the Virginia Continentals before they marched south, and he assumed command of the Virginia forces over Muhlenberg while he remained in Virginia.[158] Once the Virginia Continentals were ready, Steuben was to lead them to Greene. Greene left Virginia in late November and joined the Southern Army at Charlotte, North Carolina, on December 2.

Following the British defeat at King's Mountain on October 7, General Cornwallis canceled his advance into North Carolina and marched to Winnsboro, South Carolina. General Gates moved with the Southern Army to Charlotte while Morgan's light infantry corps marched thirteen miles south to New Providence. Greene found the Southern Army at Charlotte in the most destitute condition. The Virginians led by Colonel Buford were apparently in the worst condition that he expected. "Your troops may literally be said to be naked," Greene reported to Governor Jefferson on December 6. He was "obliged to send a considerable number of them away into some secure place and warm quarters, until they can be furnished with clothing."[159] Many men of Colonel Buford's Battalion had been left at Hillsborough in November due to lack of supplies, and only those who were the most fit and well equipped were marched to Charlotte. Buford himself was sick and stationed at Salisbury, leaving the command of the battalion to Major Thomas Ridley. Greene blamed the low morale and condition of the men not on Gates but on Jefferson and the state government. Greene wrote:

> *No man will think himself bound to fight the battles of a state that leaves him to perish for want of covering; nor can you inspire a soldier with the sentiment of pride whilst his situation renders him more an object of pity than envy. The life of a soldier in its best state is subject to innumerable hardships, but where they are aggravated by a want of provision and clothing his condition becomes intolerable, nor can men long contend with such complicated difficulties and distress.... The article of clothing is but a small part of the expense in raising, equipping, and subsisting an army, and yet on this alone the whole benefit of their service depends. I wish the State to view this matter in its true point of light; some may think it is urged for the sake of military parade, but be assured you raise men in vain unless you clothe, arm, and equip them properly for the field.*[160]

General Steuben also acknowledged the need for properly supplied troops to go south. Colonel John Green had arrived at Chesterfield Courthouse after Leslie's Raid and assumed command of Gaskins' old battalion, with Lieutenant Colonel Samuel Hawes and Major Thomas Hill attached to his command. Steuben focused on arming and clothing Green's battalion before the other Virginia Continentals to send them south. Colonel Green made sure to place the most experienced officers under his command to lead his companies. To add to their ranks, soldiers were again pulled from the First Virginia State Regiment. Unlike Buford's Battalion, these state soldiers were placed not into companies commanded by state officers but with the Continentals and were considered transferred to Continental service.[161] Green's Battalion was issued short blue jackets with red facings, overalls, new muskets and knapsacks. Blankets again became an issue. Steuben had hoped to send Green's Battalion south on December 10 but found that only 60 of the 400 men had blankets. Steuben was able to gather enough blankets for 160 men.[162] The best-supplied men from other companies were transferred to Green's Battalion, and on December 13, 1780, Green led 400 Continentals to join the Southern Army.[163]

In the first two days of the southward march, twenty-five men from Green's Battalion deserted. One of those deserters was Private John Adams. Adams was a veteran of the First Virginia State Regiment who had enlisted for the duration of the war in 1777. Adams deserted to Chesterfield Courthouse and then deserted from Chesterford, possibly to stay with relatives in Goochland County.[164] He was joined in desertion from Green's Battalion by James Jordan of Spotsylvania County and Elisha Hanson of Culpeper County. Steuben sent twenty-five more recruits from Chesterfield Courthouse to

Major General Friedrich Wilhelm Augustus, Baron von Steuben (1730–1794), by Ralph Earl (American, 1751–1801), circa 1786. *Gift of Mrs. Paul Moore in memory of her nephew Howard Melville Hanna, Jr., B.S. 1931, Yale University Art Gallery.*

replace them, including Evans Archer, a freed man of color who was enlisted from along the North Carolina border.[165] Colonel Green's Battalion joined the Southern Army near the Cheraw Hills in South Carolina in January 1781. Despite the issues of supplies and desertions, the Virginia Continental Line was beginning to become a semiorganized fighting force again. The campaigns of 1781 would stretch their ranks and test the discipline that Muhlenberg and Steuben instilled in them at Chesterfield Courthouse.

Chapter 4

# REEMERGENCE OF THE VIRGINIA LINE

## Battle of Cowpens

By December 1780, the area around Charlotte, North Carolina, was devoid of adequate forage and supplies for the Americans. British, Loyalist and American troops had been passing through the town and the region since the summer, and the countryside was picked clean. General Gates had planned to set up winter quarters near the town and had begun to construct winter huts when General Greene arrived. Greene's Army consisted of roughly 950 Continentals and 1,500 militiamen fit for service.[166] Greene spent his first month in command setting up supply posts throughout North Carolina, implementing discipline and sending officers to explore all the river systems north of Charlotte to the North Carolina border. This gave Greene an accurate picture of the terrain in which he would campaign. The issue of supplies convinced Greene to split his smaller force in the face of the British force to make it easier to feed the men. Rather than retreat and lose support in the southern region of North Carolina, Greene led a portion of his army to Hick's Creek (Cheraws), South Carolina, to supply his main force and threaten British outposts in eastern South Carolina.[167] General Morgan was sent to the backcountry with his "Flying Army" to threaten British outposts there and obtain food for the light infantry and dragoons led by Colonel William Washington.

Captain Andrew Wallace led his company of Virginia Continentals with Morgan's force. Andrew Wallace began his military service with Captain

Mathew Arbuckle when Virginians erected Fort Randolph at Point Pleasant (in modern-day West Virginia) in the fall of 1775. He remained in service with Captain Arbuckle until the spring of 1777, when he was commissioned as a captain in the Twelfth Virginia Regiment. The Wallaces, who lived along the mountains in Augusta County, were a family of soldiers. Andrew's brothers Adam and John had also been commissioned as officers in the Twelfth Virginia.[168] Lieutenant John Wallace, however, never went into battle with his brother Andrew. John died of smallpox in Philadelphia in August 1777. Both Adam and Andrew served as captains in the Twelfth Virginia and were sent south with Colonel Buford in 1780. Adam was with Buford at the Waxhaws Massacre and was killed fighting with an espontoon in hand against Lieutenant Colonel Banastre Tarleton's dragoons.[169] Andrew was twenty-four years old in 1781, a veteran of five years, and had lost two brothers along with his former regiment. This undoubtedly had some effect on Wallace's mental state and made him more cautious than other young officers. He had also taken a companion while in North Carolina. After the war, Lieutenant Colonel John Eagar Howard wrote that Wallace had "formed a connexion with a vile woman of the camp" and that the unnamed woman often accompanied Wallace on guard and other military duties and seemed miserable when she was not around him.[170] Wallace was not the only soldier who fell in love while in the Carolinas. Private Henry Emerson, a veteran soldier from Spotsylvania County, married a local woman named Nancy Neal on January 10, 1781, just a week before he and the rest of his company fought at the Battle of Cowpens.[171] Wallace was joined by veteran officers Lieutenant Conway Oldham, Lieutenant Thomas Miller and Ensign Elisha King to assist in commanding the company.

To counter Morgan's movements in the backcountry, General Cornwallis dispatched Lieutenant Colonel Tarleton with 1,150 men and two pieces of artillery to pursue Morgan and prevent any further raids by the Americans. By the night of January 16, 1781, Morgan had pulled his forces back to a place known as the Cowpens, about six miles from the Broad River. South Carolina militia joined Morgan's command and brought his force to roughly 1,900 men with no artillery. Morgan was determined to make his stand there and let Tarleton come to him. Cattle were brought on the morning of January 16 and slaughtered to feed the men fresh beef, which was a morale boost, as they had abandoned their food days earlier.[172] Morgan went around the different fires set by the men, encouraging them. In comparison, Tarleton's British and Loyalist troops were on the march through the cold night and did not rest.

The American Continentals were eager to face Tarleton in battle again. For the Maryland and Delaware Continentals, the memory of the Camden defeat five months before was still fresh. Private Henry Wells of Captain Kirkwood's Delaware Company had three cousins captured by the British there (only one returned home from imprisonment), and it was Tarleton's dragoons who helped scatter the American forces there. For the men of Captain Wallace's Company, the Waxhaws Massacre was their motivation. Captain Wallace had lost one of his brothers and several friends in the battle. Private William Jewell still bore the scars of Waxhaws. Jewell, who served under Captain Adam Wallace at Waxhaws, had his thumb shot off and was wounded in the chest by a bayonet and in the arm and head by a sword.[173] He escaped captivity after only a few months and by December 1780 was back in service in Greene's Army, where he volunteered to go with Captain Wallace. Private Robert Owls, a freed man of color from Princess Anne County, was also slightly wounded in the head by a sword at Waxhaws.[174] Other Waxhaws survivors were in the ranks, and the other soldiers undoubtedly heard the stories from those veterans.

On the morning of the battle at Cowpens on January 17, Captain Wallace and his men were formed on the right flank of the second American line. Morgan set up a trap for Tarleton along the hills of the Cowpens. Riflemen were placed in front to force Tarleton's men into line and then fall back into the first main line of Morgan's forces, which consisted of militia from North and South Carolina. The second main line, which consisted of Virginia militia and Continental infantry, was 150 yards behind the militia. Captain Wallace's Continentals were placed on the right of the line, with a small company of North Carolina state troops in support. Captain Edmund Tate is believed to have commanded the temporary battalion consisting of Wallace's Continentals and Virginia militia and state troops.[175] Captain Tate was a militia officer and yet was placed in command over Captain Wallace, who was a Continental officer. Especially in Virginia, Continental officers usually took seniority over militia officers. The Maryland and Delaware Continentals were placed in the center under Lieutenant Colonel John Eager Howard (who commanded the whole second line as well), and Major Francis Triplett commanded another battalion of Virginia militia.

As Tarleton's men arrived on the field, the battle opened with the riflemen, as Morgan had planned. The riflemen then fell back to the militia line, with British troops following behind them. As the sun rose, the British formed line with the British Legion infantry on the right side of the road and the Seventh Regiment (Fusiliers) on the left side of the road facing the Americans, with

"Battle of Cowpens—Conflict Between Cols. Washington and Tarleton." *Miriam and Ira D. Wallach Division of Art, Prints and Photographs: Print Collection, New York Public Library Digital Collections.*

the Seventeenth Dragoons posted on the right flank and the British Legion dragoons on the left. With the firing of the two three-pounders posted in the center, the British gave three huzzahs and advanced on the militia.[176] As in many of his engagements, Tarleton planned to rely on a quick attack with sword and bayonet to win the day; this tactic had worked before in several engagements in the South, including Waxhaws. The British Legion infantry led the attack, as the Seventh Regiment and Seventy-First Regiment (Fraser's Highlanders) mixed together and struggled to deploy. After firing three to five shots (depending on the account), the militia began to fall back. The British had been trained to follow American riflemen closely when attacking them to prevent them from reloading. Rifles were slower to reload than muskets, and with no bayonets, the riflemen were at a disadvantage in close combat. This tactic allowed for the American militia to fire their volleys while taking few casualties from British fire up to that point in the battle.

As the militia fell back, the second line, including Wallace's Virginians, made gaps to allow the militia to pass through, as ordered by Morgan. Retreating soldiers could create disorder and panic by breaking up the formation of troops stationed behind them. The Marylanders had experienced disaster at the Battle of Brandywine in 1777 for the same reason and again when the militia broke at Camden. Morgan, an experienced officer, was not going to risk this at Cowpens. Wallace and his men, though not in the direct line of fire, had received artillery fire from the two British guns, and stray musket shots still fell with some effect on the line, though the casualties remained light.[177] The British saw the solid line of American troops, and Tarleton halted his men for a few minutes to reform their lines before ordering them forward again. The Seventh Regiment and the British Legion infantry had advanced up to this point in open order, meaning that there was space between their files, but now they closed these spaces as they went up against what they saw as regular and veteran troops. The Seventh Regiment went straight against Howard's Continentals, while the men of Tate's Battalion,

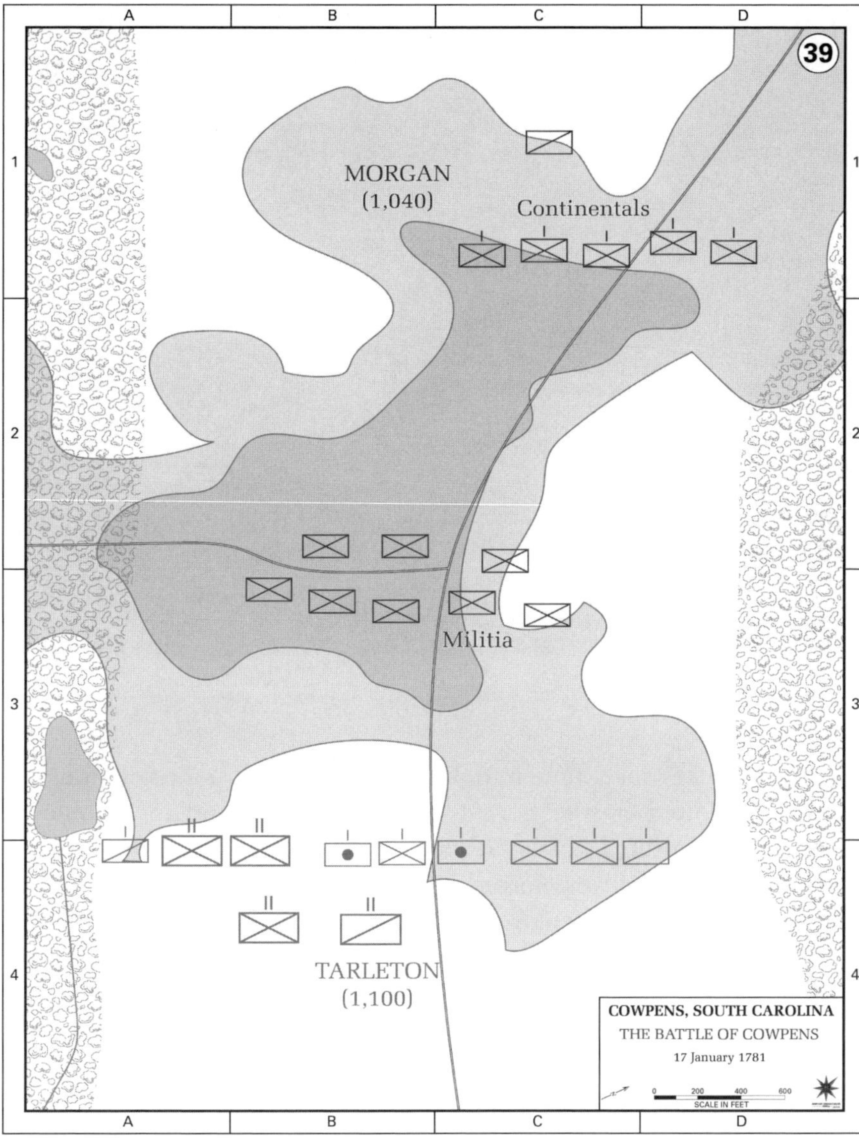


*Opposite*: Mass grave of Virginians at Waxhaws battlefield. *Author's collection.*

*Above*: Initial deployments of British and American troops at Cowpens. Captain Wallace's company was on the extreme right of the Continentals. *Courtesy of the United States Military Academy Department of History.*

View of the American lines from the British center at Cowpens. *Author's collection.*

including Wallace's men, fired into the ranks of the British Legion dragoons, who were followed by the Seventy-First Regiment, and for a time did not receive heavy fire, which prevented heavy casualties at this point.[178] American skirmishers were forced back by the Legion dragoons, and the Seventy-First Regiment deployed facing Wallace's men. The Highlanders were determined to fight hard against the Continentals, as they reportedly were given orders to take no prisoners.[179] Wallace's men stood their ground alongside the Virginia State Troops led by Captain John Lawson on their left. The North Carolina State Troops that were stationed to Wallace's right fell back when the Legion cavalry went around the right flank to engage the cavalry led by Colonel Washington. Howard saw this and the advance of the Seventy-First Regiment as the attack that could destroy the line and turn the battle at Cowpens into a British victory. Howard thus ordered Wallace to refuse the line, or turn his company back into a ninety-degree angle to face the Seventy-First Regiment's attack. It was at this point that the battle entered its most pivotal phase.

Captain Wallace ordered his men to about-face, or turn around, and wheel into line. This maneuver would allow the company to swing like a gate by the "hinge" to the right and form again to face the enemy. In the execution of this maneuver, however, Colonel Howard saw Wallace's company not wheeling but retreating in line. The confusion of this order has some different explanations. Howard claimed that Wallace had "lost all sense of the character of an officer" and was in a miserable state of mind on the morning of the battle, which Howard attributed to the absence of his companion from camp.[180] His "miserable state of mind" could also be attributed to the loss of two of his brothers; it may be that in later engagements, he feared his own death, having escaped it over the five years of his service. A practical reason for the misunderstanding of the order may have been the noise of battle, and the confusion may not have been Wallace's but that of his subordinate officer. As Wallace gave the order to wheel right, which would have been "To the right wheel, march," the Seventy-First Regiment fired a volley into the ranks of the Virginians. On the other end of Wallace's company, Lieutenant Conway Oldham, Wallace's subordinate, would have waited for the order "march" to execute the order. In the noise of battle, Oldham may have only heard the order "march" and ordered the same. The men then moved forward, and perhaps Wallace was unsure

Position of Captain Wallace's Company facing toward the British advance. *Author's collection.*

Over this ground the Seventy-First Regiment advanced; this was the direction Captain Wallace's company was supposed to face if not for the misunderstood order. *Author's collection.*

how to fix it or was confused himself about what was going on. In the same volley, Captain John Lawson was killed while at the head of the Virginia State Troops company, and Lieutenant Thomas Taylor took command. He saw the retreat of Wallace's Company, assumed a retreat had been ordered and fired a volley before he retired as well.[181] This caused every company on the line to do the same.

No matter the reason for the misunderstood order, the fact remained that the American line was beginning to retreat, and Tarleton determined to finish off Morgan's force and win the day. There was no confusion in the American ranks, however, as they fell back in good order and continued to reload as they marched. Morgan and Howard rallied the men roughly one hundred yards behind the original line and then turned toward the British. Once faced about toward the Seventy-First, Wallace's men began to fire into the ranks of the Highlanders at a range of thirty yards, and the rest of the line did the same. This volley stopped the British attack, which had already become disordered in the final charge. Colonel Washington's cavalry then started the attack on the shattered ranks of the Seventy-First, while Howard

Position of Captain Wallace's company after rallying, facing the charging British. *Author's collection.*

Colonel Washington at the Battle of Cowpens. *Miriam and Ira D. Wallach Division of Art, Prints and Photographs: Print Collection, New York Public Library Digital Collections.*

Part of the Cowpens Monument. Captain Wallace and Lieutenant Oldham are excluded from the names of officers on the monument. *Author's collection.*

ordered the Continentals to charge into the British ranks. Wallace and his men joined in the attack with bayonets and followed closely behind the Seventy-First, capturing most of them. In less than thirty minutes, General Morgan and his men had won a major victory against Tarleton and his men. Tarleton had lost over 900 men killed, wounded or captured in addition to the two three-pounders he took onto the field. Tarleton himself barely escaped after a personal fight with Colonel Washington and his cavalry. Morgan lost 149 Americans killed and wounded in the short battle.

Four men from Captain Wallace's Company are accounted for through pension applications as having been wounded at Cowpens. Private John Brownlee, a veteran of three years, was shot in the cheek and thigh when the Seventy-First Regiment fired its volley before retreating. He was later declared unfit for service and returned home to Augusta County in the spring.[182] Private Thomas Crawford, a veteran of the Eighth Virginia Regiment, was wounded in the arm and thigh, retired from military service and then moved to Frederick County.[183] Jacob Taylor received a bayonet wound from a soldier in the Seventy-First, and Rockingham County orphan William Warren was wounded in the left thigh but returned to service in the spring.[184] Lieutenant Thomas Miller was recognized for his actions in the battle, as was Ensign Elisha King. Wallace was left out of General Morgan's official report, as was Lieutenant Oldham.

## Race to the Dan

The Virginia Continentals who remained with General Greene in January 1781 did not experience the victory that Captain Wallace and his men did but rather a solemn execution. Private Thomas Chapman of the First Maryland Regiment was court-martialed for desertion for the third time in seven months and was found guilty on December 28, 1780. The court sentenced him to death by firing squad. On January 5, 1781, the execution was viewed by the entire Continental force, including the Virginians belonging to Colonel Buford's Battalion. Lieutenant Albert Russell, acting adjutant of Buford's Battalion, read the sentence before the execution and the event set the example that desertion would not be tolerated in General Greene's Southern Army.[185] Colonel John Green's Battalion arrived in camp five days later and was brigaded with Buford's Battalion, commanded by Major Thomas Ridley. Brigadier General Isaac Huger was placed in command of the new Virginia Brigade, which now consisted of roughly seven hundred officers and men. Companies were reorganized as well. Captain John Marks returned to Virginia, and most of his men were transferred to the company commanded by Captain John Anderson in Green's Battalion.[186] Two officers also left Buford's Battalion: both Captains Thomas Bell and Samuel Lapsley resigned their commissions because their parent regiment (Gist's Additional Regiment) was disbanded on January 1, 1781, and they were apparently not respected by the other officers of the Virginia Continental Line. The Additional Continental Regiments were raised separately from their native states, and state continental officers did not wish to be commanded by men who were not part of their respective line regiments. General Greene accepted the resignations of both officers.[187]

In addition, at least one officer was upset by Greene's reorganization of officers. Lieutenant William Eppes had been sent south with Colonel Buford in September 1780 in command of a company, and Colonel William Davies had apparently been appointed "captain" without an accompanying commission. Greene arrived and found officers acting as captains and calling themselves "Captain" without the commissions. Greene ordered this to cease on January 18 and the officers to assume the rank of their most recent commission, with Continental commissions taking rank over state and militia commissions, respectively. Lieutenant Eppes complained to General Greene, claiming he was entitled to a promotion, and though he had no official commission, Colonel Davies had appointed him as a captain. General Greene responded that he was not denying Eppes the right of promotion but Eppes should wait to be promoted to captain rather than assume the rank. Eppes tried to resign, and Greene attempted to guilt him, writing on January 21 that "no officer can leave the army with reputation under such circumstances, and more especially at a time when his Country has the most occasion for his services." Eppes did not care for Greene's response and submitted his resignation the following day. Greene accepted his resignation, having written to Eppes earlier, "I shall sooner loose an officer than introduce precedent which can not be warranted either by reason or custom."[188]

Brigadier General Isaac Huger. *Miriam and Ira D. Wallach Division of Art, Prints and Photographs: Print Collection, New York Public Library Digital Collections.*

General Cornwallis was deeply upset by the defeat at Cowpens. On January 19, after receiving 1,200 reinforcements from General Alexander Leslie, Cornwallis marched with 2,500 men to take back the prisoners captured at Cowpens and destroy Morgan's Flying Army. Morgan, however, knew this was a possibility and had begun to march the day before Cornwallis marched out of Winnsboro. General Greene left General Huger in command of the Continentals at Hick's Creek to go meet with Morgan in North Carolina around the same time. Morgan and Greene met at Gilbert Town (Rutherfordton), North Carolina on January 30 and decided that Morgan would continue to move his Flying Army toward Salisbury, North Carolina, after delaying Cornwallis along the

Catawba River. Greene also sent orders to General Huger and ordered the Continentals to rendezvous with Morgan at Salisbury. Thus began the famous "Race to the Dan," in which Greene raced toward the Virginia border while Cornwallis followed, attempting to catch up to Greene. The American forces were united at Guilford Courthouse on February 9, where General Morgan retired from military service due to his health, and Colonel Otho Williams of the Maryland Line was placed in command of the new light infantry detachment of the Southern Army. Howard's Light Infantry Corps remained, with another company of Virginia Continentals led by Lieutenant Philip Huffman, was detached from Green's and Buford's Battalions and attached to Howard's Corps. Huffman's addition brought Howard's strength to 280 total.[189] Huffman's Company mostly cooperated with Captain Robert Kirkwood and his company of Delaware Continentals.

On February 10, General Greene ordered his army toward Boyd's and Irwin's Ferries over the Dan River in Virginia. At the same time, Greene ordered Colonel Williams to take the light infantry, sixty Virginia riflemen, Colonel Washington's First and Third Continental Dragoons and Lee's Legion seven miles west of Guilford Courthouse to distract Cornwallis' force from following him. Over the next four days, Cornwallis trailed Colonel Williams' force while Williams trailed Greene. General Greene, with the assistance of Lieutenant Colonel Edward Carrington of Virginia, started to ferry his men across the swollen Dan River on February 13, while Williams' force crossed on the evening of February 14—not without some hardship. Williams and his men were forced to cover roughly thirty miles to Irwin's Ferry in one day but were safely across the river by midnight. British forces led by Lieutenant Colonel Tarleton arrived at Irwin's Ferry only seven hours later.[190]

## Arnold's Raid

While Greene's and Morgan's forces were marching across the Carolinas, the Virginia Continentals under General Steuben in Virginia went through their own trials. The departure of Colonel Green's Battalion left roughly six hundred soldiers at Chesterfield Courthouse, though many were unfit for service due to lack of clothing.[191] The Continentals that Steuben found in Virginia were "in general naked and badly armed" in addition to being an organizational nightmare.[192] Many of the officers of the Virginia Continental Line were still absent from service despite having been ordered to report to Chesterfield Courthouse repeatedly by General Muhlenberg. This greatly upset General Steuben, who wrote that Virginia "Swarms with Officers & Soldiers, who under different Pretences, never join their Colors, & draw all the while their pay & Rations, commit Excesses thro' the Country, & render no Kind of Services."[193] Before Steuben could reorganize and begin to send more troops south after Green's Battalion, another British force arrived in Virginia.

In late December 1780, former American officer and now British General Benedict Arnold arrived near Hampton Roads with 1,200 soldiers to raid into Virginia. The goal of Arnold's presence in Virginia was to prevent supplies being sent to the Southern Army and stop any further trade into Virginia.[194] General Sir Henry Clinton, as well as many other British officers, saw Virginia as the lifeline of the South. All supplies and manpower must either originate or pass through Virginia to the Southern Army under General Greene. Arnold landed his forces at Hampton Roads to raid for supplies in the area, skirmishing with militia near Hampton and Warwick.[195] By January 2, Arnold and his forces had reboarded their vessels and sailed up the James River toward the state capital, Richmond. Governor Jefferson called for one-quarter of the militia from twenty counties in central Virginia to rendezvous at Petersburg in response to Arnold's raid.[196] After dispersing militia at Hood's Point, General Arnold landed at Westover Plantation and marched on Richmond.

General Steuben had believed, much like Governor Jefferson, that Arnold's real target was Petersburg and so had planned to send the Virginia Continentals at Chesterfield to guard the Continental stores that were kept there on January 2.[197] To Steuben's dismay, however, only 150 soldiers were clothed and equipped enough to take the field. They were formed into a battalion, possibly commanded by Lieutenant Colonel Richard Campbell. Once it became clear that Richmond was the target and Arnold was within twenty-five miles of the capitol, Steuben ordered the small battalion of Virginia Continentals to Westham, while the "naked troops" who remained at Chesterfield were ordered to march under Colonel Davies.[198] On January 5, General Arnold marched with 850 of his men into Richmond and, after some quick skirmishing with militia and state troops under Major Alexander Dick of the Virginia State Line, destroyed many of the public buildings, including the powder magazine and foundry. The next day, General Steuben marched with the 150-man Continental battalion and two pieces of artillery from the State Artillery to Manchester, where they were joined by 200 militiamen to prevent Arnold from crossing the James River.[199] After Arnold left Richmond, some Virginia Continentals were sent, possibly with Captain Frederick Woodson of the Second Virginia State Regiment, to go with Colonel John Nicholas to harass Arnold's force. The Virginia Continentals were involved in at least one skirmish near Shirley's Plantation, a neighboring property to Westover. Private Tapley Lightfoot was present for the skirmish and claimed that Colonel Davies was present as well and acted with "great cowardice."[200] This skirmish may have included the Queen's Rangers, as Private John Carson recalled being involved in a skirmish with Loyalist troops before he was marched to North Carolina.[201]

Other Virginia Continental troops were sent after Arnold when he moved toward Suffolk, and at least one company of soldiers was sent toward that location. The Continentals acted as light infantry for Steuben and performed scouting missions against the British. Some of the Virginians took advantage of being close to British lines to desert. In one night, Frederick Snider of Montgomery County, Archibald and Jonathan Praytor and two others left their muskets against a tree and deserted from their posts on picket. Fearing that they had given information to the enemy, the Virginia Continentals were forced to move camp.[202]

After about two weeks in the field, General Steuben ordered the remaining Virginia Continentals back to Chesterfield Courthouse. Once back in Chesterfield, with Virginia militia and state troops holding Arnold's force at Portsmouth, Steuben set to sending the next battalion of Virginia Continentals to General Greene's Army. New blue jackets faced in red were made for 400 men, to be organized into a battalion commanded by Lieutenant Colonel Richard Campbell. The majority of the battalion consisted of eighteen-month recruits, though some had combat experience. Again, state soldiers were pulled into the ranks to fill the vacancies, including William Loyd, who was transferred from the Virginia State Garrison Regiment stationed in Richmond.[203] On February 24, 1781, Colonel Campbell's Battalion marched out of Chesterfield Courthouse to join Greene's Army, leaving roughly 150 soldiers with Steuben to form the nucleus of a new battalion he hoped to organize in the spring. Steuben and others hoped that another battalion would be sent to join Greene later that spring, but those men were not destined to march south until a full year later.

## The Battle of Guilford Courthouse

After resting for a week in Halifax County, Virginia, General Greene and his force crossed the Dan River on February 22 and marched against General Cornwallis at Hillsborough. Over the next three weeks, the two armies never stayed in one place for long. The Virginians under Captain Wallace and Lieutenant Huffman continued to march with Colonel Williams' light infantry battalion, skirmishing with British forces alongside Virginia riflemen and militia from North Carolina. They engaged British troops led by Lieutenant Colonel Tarleton along Alamance Creek on March 2, where they covered the retreat of militia and riflemen from a bayonet charge of the Thirty-Third Regiment. In the Battle of Wetzell's Mill on March 7, Cornwallis attempted to cut off Williams and his advance force from Greene's main army, which was gathering at Guilford Courthouse, but Williams moved his force faster. The riflemen and militia again fought a delaying action while the Continentals crossed Reedy Creek, and the Continentals covered their retreat in turn. The Continentals repulsed the first British attempt to cross the creek, but the second attempt was successful as the Thirty-Third Regiment and the British Guards Light Infantry forced their way across the creek. Williams, despite the pressure, was able to successfully withdraw his force and prevent disaster. At least one Virginian was wounded at Wetzell's Mill. Private Ephraim Lands of Captain Wallace's Company was disabled after he was accidentally shot in the hand.[204]

Engagements such as Alamance Creek and Wetzell's Mill led up the major battle at Guilford Courthouse on March 15. General Greene used a tactic like the one General Morgan used with success at Cowpens two months before. The Americans were formed into three lines. The first line consisted largely of the North Carolina Militia, with Captain Wallace's Virginia Light Infantry Company on the left flank along with Virginia riflemen and Lee's Legion and, on the right flank, Lieutenant Huffman's Light Infantry Company. Huffman's Company cooperated with Captain Kirkwood's Delaware Continentals in the battle.[205] The second line consisted of the Virginia Militia, divided into two brigades and led by Brigadier Generals Edward Stevens and Robert Lawson. The third line consisted of the Continentals of Greene's Army. The Maryland Brigade was led by Colonel Otho Williams and consisted of the reorganized First and Second Maryland Regiments. Brigadier General Isaac Huger commanded the Virginia Brigade, though the composition of the brigade is confusing.

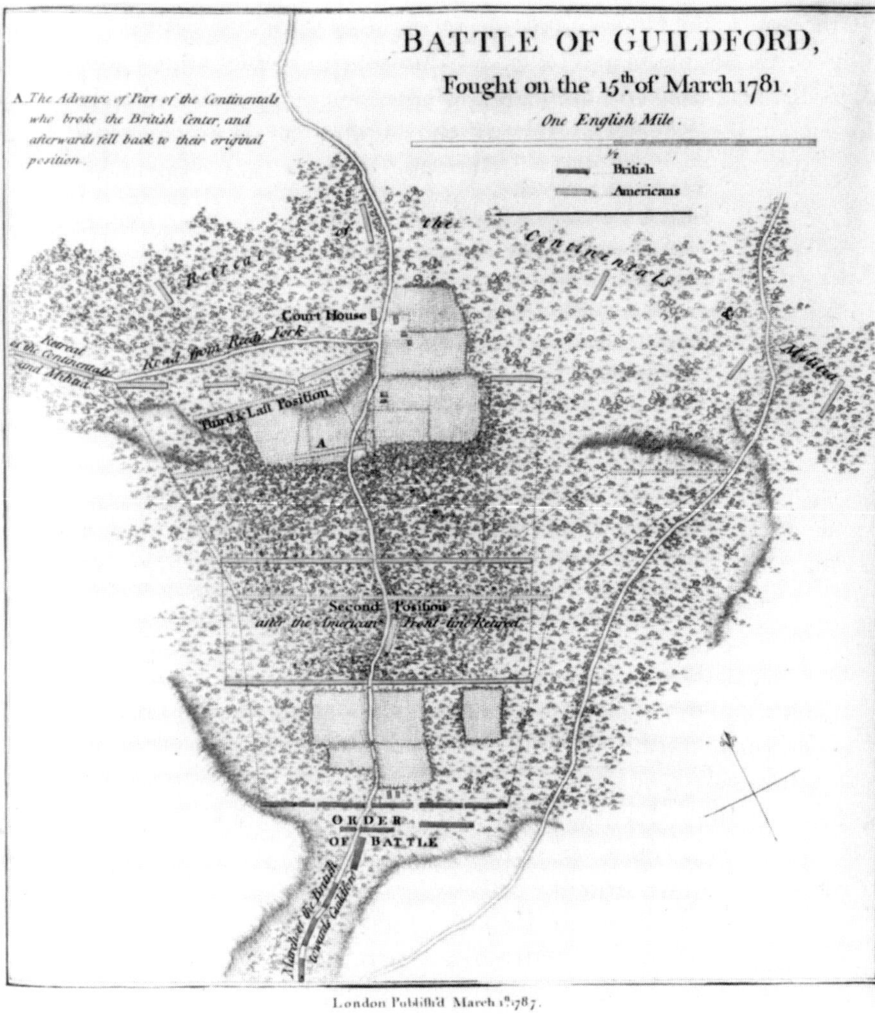


"Battle of Guildford, fought on the 15th of March 1781." *Library of Congress.*

In contemporary publications, the Virginia Brigade is divided into only two battalions, led by Colonel John Green and Lieutenant Colonel Samuel Hawes. Other accounts, however, place three battalions of Virginia Continentals on the third line at Guilford Courthouse. Although Colonel Buford was no longer in the field commanding, Buford's Battalion was also present on the battlefield. Private Philip Wolfenberger, an eighteen-month volunteer from Shenandoah County, recalled in 1819 that Major Thomas Ridley was still in command of the battalion at Guilford Courthouse. In all,

110 more Virginia Continentals are recorded as belonging to five companies in Buford's Battalion at Guilford Courthouse. Though the soldiers said Major Ridley was in command, records indicate Lieutenant Colonel Samuel Hawes had most likely taken command of the battalion; accordingly, this unit will be referred to as Hawes' Battalion. Lieutenant Colonel Campbell's Battalion joined Greene's army on March 11, and based on the recollections of Lieutenant Colonel Henry Lee, the men of Campbell's Battalion were dispersed to the battalions of Green and Hawes. Lee's account may refer to the April 1781 reorganization, but since General Greene was on the move when Campbell joined him and no letters confirm any reorganization before the Battle of Guilford Courthouse, Lee may have confused the timing of the reorganization. Another indication is from the field return of the Southern Army recorded on March 13, only two days before Guilford Courthouse. It is recorded with the return that there was "no regular regiment" in either brigade of Continental troops (referring to the Maryland and Virginia Line) and that they operated as different detachments.[206] Each of the detachments had a sergeant major and a quartermaster sergeant. Records indicate that the Virginia Brigade had three sergeant majors and three quartermaster sergeants, in addition to three adjutants in service, on March 13, 1781, which indicates three battalions. In comparison, the Maryland Brigade went into Guilford Courthouse with two battalions and reported two sergeant majors and two quartermaster sergeants on March 13.[207] Including the strength of Huffman's and Wallace's light infantry companies, the Virginia Continentals had 909 officers and men, roughly one-fifth of the Southern Army at Guilford Courthouse.[208]

As the British attack began around noon, the North Carolina Militia fired a volley from a distance of 140 yards, and many panicked as 2,000 British and Hessian troops advanced in their front. The Virginians of Wallace and Huffman, however, stood their ground alongside Virginia riflemen and Delaware Continentals to fire another volley at roughly forty yards against the advancing enemy. As the British swept away the remaining North Carolinians, Captain Wallace with his company, the men of Lee's Legion and Virginia riflemen to the southeast led by Lieutenant Colonel Henry Lee fell back toward the left flank of the Virginia militia.

These troops soon engaged a battalion of British Guard infantry in thick woods that broke up company formations. The Virginians fell on both flanks of the British Guards, and only the timely arrival of the Von Bose Regiment of Hessians prevented total disaster for the Guards. Captain Wallace's Continentals engaged in the heavy fighting against the Hessians and Guards,

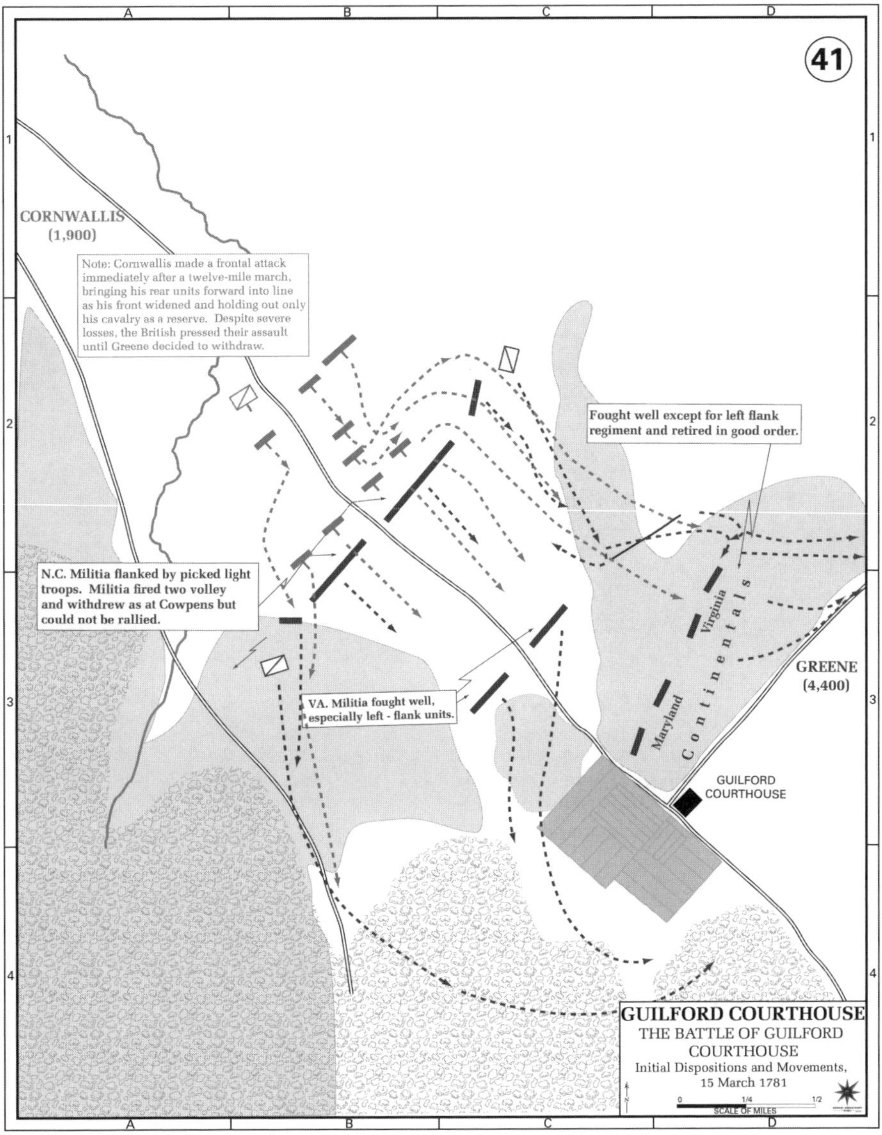


Map of the Battle of Guilford Courthouse. *Author's collection.*

with Captain Wallace commanding from behind a tree. On the morning of the battle, Wallace expressed "a mournful presage" that he was destined to be killed that day and found shelter behind a tree "with some indications of alarm."[209] He was reproached, most likely by Lieutenant Colonel Lee, and immediately left his shelter, only to be shot down moments later. Wallace

*Above*: Site of the Guilford Courthouse. *Author's collection.*

*Opposite*: Lee's cavalry skirmishing at the Battle of Guilford. *Miriam and Ira D. Wallach Division of Art, Prints and Photographs: Print Collection, New York Public Library Digital Collections.*

became the third of the Wallace brothers of Augusta to die in the American Revolution. Colonel Lee eventually pulled his command out, along with the remainder of Wallace's company, while the riflemen continued to fight until cut up by Tarleton's dragoons.

On the American right flank, Lieutenant Huffman's Company continued to fight alongside Kirkwood's Delawareans against British light infantry and Hessian Jägers. Huffman and his men rallied alongside the Virginia Militia and fought a running engagement with the British and Hessian riflemen.[210] Eventually the men were driven back to the third line, though Huffman was not with them. Private Alexander Stewart fought alongside Lieutenant Huffman and was present to see Huffman shot and killed before the men retreated.[211] The British advanced quickly, capturing Stewart and other members of the company as they fled through the woods. Huffman's men rallied with the Delawareans alongside the Virginians under Huger, where the Virginians earned their nickname Hell-Fired Blues.

When it comes to the third line at Guilford Courthouse, the focus has often been on the fighting between the Second Battalion of British Guards and the First Maryland Regiment and Colonel Washington's dragoons, but the Virginians to their right were engaged in fighting as well. Lieutenant Colonel Hawes' Battalion was formed directly to the left of the First Maryland, with Campbell's Battalion making up the center and Green's Battalion on the right flank of the brigade. Huffman's and Kirkwood's companies reformed

*This page*: Position of Captain Wallace's company on the left flank of the first line. *Author's collection.*

These woods are similar to those that Captain Wallace and Lieutenant Huffman's company fought through on both flanks of the second line. *Author's collection.*

to the right of Green's Battalion and continued to fight the British Guards light infantry and Jägers. Some Virginia militiamen, after retreating from the second line, rallied with Campbell's Battalion.[212] The main opponents of the Virginians were the Thirty-Third Regiment, alongside the British Guards light infantry and Jägers.

The Thirty-Third Regiment advanced from the woods in the direction of the two six-pounders located in the middle of the Virginia Brigade. The two guns, commanded by Captain-Lieutenant Ebenezer Finley, were visible to the Thirty-Third Regiment, led by Lieutenant Colonel James Webster. The Virginians under General Huger were likely concealed by the thick woods on the high ground, and thus Webster may have not seen them when he led the Thirty-Third into a bayonet charge against them. Webster's hope for victory in this charge was short-lived as case shot from Finley's guns tore into his ranks. At the same time, Webster began to take heavy musket fire from the First Maryland on the right, Hawes' and Campbell's Virginians in the front and Green's Virginians on the left. As quickly as the Thirty-Third crossed the swale toward the third line, they fell back. In the repulse,

Generals Greene and Huger apparently wanted to take advantage of the situation and ordered an advance. "We were ordered up to their assistance," Private Lewis Griffin of Campbell's Battalion recalled. "At this juncture the battle became bloody, each party making an obstinate stand."[213] The attack, however, was not complete, and the Virginians returned to their former position. Colonel William R. Davie, who served as Greene's commissary general, recalled that the Virginians were "repeatedly led up to action by General Greene in person, and could not stand the fire of the enemy."[214] General Huger rode along the line encouraging the Virginians forward and was wounded in the right hand by a musket ball. He caught his falling sword with his left hand, wrapped his hand in a handkerchief and continued to encourage the men.[215]

The Virginia and Delaware light infantrymen also followed in the attack against the British light infantry and Jägers. Sergeant Major William Seymour offered some explanation of why the counterattack was not successful:

> *They pursued them up a very steep hill, almost inaccessible, till observing the enemy, who lay concealed in ambush, rise up, and pouring in a very heavy fire on them, in which they were obliged to retreat, having suffered very much by the last fire of the enemy.*[216]

*This page and opposite*: The area around the left flank of Hawes' Battalion on the third line. *Author's collection.*

The fighting along the right flank became sporadic infantry fire while the Maryland Brigade and the Continental dragoons, led by Colonel Washington, engaged in heavy fighting against the Second Battalion of British Guards. After heavy fighting, both Maryland regiments were forced from the field, and the right flank of the Virginians was exposed to the attack of the British Guards, as well as the Twenty-Third Regiment and the Second Battalion of the Seventy-First Regiment. General Greene realized that his position was compromised and he needed to get his remaining soldiers off the field. Colonel Green's Battalion was pulled from the line, stationed across the Reedy Fork Road and ordered to act as the rear guard of the Southern Army. Hawes' and Campbell's Battalions continued to hold their position as they were attacked on the flank, and the Thirty-Third Regiment, reformed by Lieutenant Colonel Webster, attacked the front again. While one Virginian mortally wounded Webster, Hawes and Campbell eventually were forced to take their battalions off the field. Private Edward Moody of Hawes' Battalion claimed that he personally fired eighteen rounds in the battle before his battalion was ordered to withdraw.[217] The conditions of the retreat are disputed, though it appears that the Virginia Brigade was able to get off the field in decent order. Major Charles Magill, acting as aide-de-camp to General Huger, wrote to Governor Jefferson the next day that "never was ground contested for with greater Obstinacy, and never were Troops drawn off in better order."[218] Colonel Green's Battalion was the last American unit off the field at Guilford Courthouse, with a company of Virginians led by Lieutenant Matthew Rhea successfully repulsing an attack of Tarleton's dragoons.[219]

The Battle of Guilford Courthouse was the first time that a large contingent of the Virginia Continental Line had participated in a battle in ten months. The Virginia Brigade reported 29 killed, 40 wounded and 39 missing, for a total of 108, or about 11.8 percent of the brigade's strength. These casualty figures included the losses of the light infantry companies of Huffman and Wallace. Forty of the casualties from the Virginia Line have been identified as killed, wounded or captured in the battle through pension applications. Based on the surviving records, the heaviest casualties came from Buford's Battalion (26 confirmed casualties), followed by Campbell's Battalion (9 confirmed) and Green's Battalion (5 confirmed). Sergeant Robert Clark, one of three brothers present on the battlefield, was shot through the abdomen and was disabled by the musket ball passing near his right hip, weakening it.[220] Private Rawleigh Christian of Buford's Battalion (a veteran of five years) was wounded twice in the battle; the first was a wound to his left hand

Two six-pounder guns, similar to the guns of Lieutenant Finley's command stationed between Hawes' and Campbell's Battalions. *Author's collection.*

that broke a finger and "rendered that hand almost useless," and the second was a musket ball that struck his right thigh just above his knee and had to be extracted by a surgeon.[221] Private Joseph Monk of Buford's Battalion lost his left eye, and Sergeant Major Christopher McCannon of Campbell's Battalion was disabled by a musket ball wound in his left arm.[222]

Despite the Americans having to give up the field and a good portion of the Virginia Continentals having been in combat for the first time, the men's morale was high, and they spoiled for another fight against Cornwallis' Army.[223] Guilford Courthouse was a tactical victory for Cornwallis, as his men held the field at the end of the day, but it was a pyrrhic victory. Cornwallis' British and Hessian soldiers were outnumbered two to one yet had forced Greene to withdraw—but at a cost of 532 killed, wounded or missing, or about 28 percent of his force.[224] Three days after the battle, Cornwallis led his army to Wilmington, North Carolina, in the hopes of being resupplied by the British Navy there. General Greene had taken over 4,400 men into the battle and reported 1,309 killed, wounded or missing. In reality, however, many of the missing were men from the North Carolina

Militia who never reported back to Greene following the battle. In addition, historians Lawrence Babits and Joshua Howard state that Greene's casualty report was 15–20 percent higher than he reported, based on pensions and other post-battle sources. The actual casualty count, considering the subtraction of the missing, was 314, or roughly 7 percent of his force.[225] The departure of the Virginia Militia, however, shortly after the battle prevented Greene from effectively pursuing Cornwallis toward Wilmington.

## Reorganization of the Virginia Brigade

Despite their performance at Guilford Courthouse, General Greene still remarked to Governor Jefferson that "the detachments also that have been sent on are greatly overrated."[226] The low number of officers in the Virginia Line in the field may have contributed to this idea, as well as the condition of their clothing and accouterments. On the March 31, 1781 field return of Greene's Army, the Virginia Brigade had one colonel, two lieutenant colonels, two majors, seven captains, one captain-lieutenant, three lieutenants and twelve ensigns. The Virginia Brigade is estimated to have had twenty-two companies split between the three battalions: six from Buford's, and eight each from Green's and Campbell's. A company of infantry, based on the regulations of the period, would have a captain, two lieutenants and one ensign as commissioned officers, four sergeants and sixty-eight enlisted men. This created a ratio of one commissioned officer to seventeen enlisted men. Based on the March 31 return, the officer-to-enlisted-men ratio would have been one to thirty-one. In addition, less than one-third of the companies were commanded by a captain. Major Magill lamented the lack of officers in the Virginia Brigade and how it may have affected the conduct of the men at Guilford Courthouse. "The Virginia Regulars with a sufficient number of Officers would have done honor to themselves," Major Magill wrote to Jefferson, and "that deficiency frequently created confusion" on the battlefield.[227] This contradicts the praise Magill gave the successful rearguard action at the battle.

General Greene had planned to reorganize the Virginia Brigade as soon as Campbell's Battalion joined the Southern Army. The battle at Guilford Courthouse and the subsequent campaigning prevented this plan from being executed until the following month. On April 4, 1781, Greene ordered General Huger, Lieutenant Colonel Campbell and Lieutenant Colonel Hawes to "form the several detachments of Virginia Troops into two Regiments of Eight Companies each."[228] The officers, sergeants and musicians would be equally distributed to the sixteen companies, which left each company with one or two commissioned officers and three or four sergeants. Equally distributed, each company would consist of roughly fifty officers and men. The two regiments were designated the First Virginia Regiment, led by Campbell, and the Second Virginia Regiment, led by Hawes.[229] Colonel John Green suffered from illness and, following the Battle of Guilford Courthouse, retired to Virginia, where he remained for the duration of the war.

Colonel Green was not the only individual from the Virginia Brigade to leave the Southern Army. Captains Abraham Kirkpatrick and Joseph Scott Jr. were also recalled to Virginia with soldiers to guard baggage and, later, command troops there. The Virginia State Line soldiers were also split up. The officers of the Virginia State Line were sent back to Virginia under Captains Thomas W. Ewell and Windsor Brown. Those soldiers who were enlisted for the duration of the war and went with Ewell and Brown were later incorporated into the First Virginia State Regiment under Lieutenant Colonel Charles Dabney (a regiment that was reorganized as Dabney's Legion in January 1782).[230] Those who were enlisted for three years or less were transferred to the Continental companies and served the remainder of their term as Continentals. In all, 1,344 officers and men were in service in the Virginia Brigade, with 830 present and fit for service. The Virginia Brigade consisted of roughly 40 percent of Greene's Southern Army as they pursued Cornwallis across North Carolina.

While encamped at Ramsey's Mill, North Carolina, General Greene not only took the time to rest and reorganize the Virginia Brigade but also developed a new strategy for winning the South. Greene wrote to General Washington on March 29 of his new plan that would change the war in the South by a march back into South Carolina. General Greene's plan put General Cornwallis in a position to make one of two choices. The first was to follow Greene into South Carolina to continue the war. The second was to let Greene march into South Carolina, allow the British and Loyalist forces there to fight Greene and continue his march toward Virginia. The second choice would risk letting South Carolina fall back into American control and losing all ground gained in 1779 and 1780. Cornwallis made the gamble to march to Virginia to join British forces there. This set the stage for both the Virginia Continentals for their campaign in the South and for the remaining Virginia Continentals under Steuben in Virginia.

Chapter 5

# A SUMMER OF MARCHING

## The Virginia Continentals in Virginia

After the departure of Campbell's Battalion in February 1781, General Steuben determined to collect more recruits to form the nucleus of another battalion at Chesterfield Courthouse. Steuben left General Muhlenberg to contain and skirmish with Arnold's force around Portsmouth while he trained and organized Continental recruits to join General Greene. Steuben, however, was not popular among the civilians and politicians of Virginia, particularly Governor Jefferson. The main point of contention was Jefferson's view on the strict observance of state laws, while Steuben, with his mind on winning the war, put military matters at the forefront and above civilian liberties. In addition, Steuben had upset officers of the Virginia Line over the reappointment of a familiar officer.

Brigadier General Weedon had disputed his rank with General Woodford starting in the spring of 1777. After the arrangement establishing the seniority of the Virginia brigadiers, Weedon found himself near the bottom of the list, with Woodford the most senior brigadier. Weedon, who had respect for Woodford from their mutual service together under Washington during the French and Indian War, objected to Woodford's appointment over him. He argued that since Woodford had resigned as colonel in 1776 but was appointed brigadier in 1777, he had given up his seniority over Weedon.[231] In response to this, Weedon attempted to resign. Like Daniel Morgan, Weedon was allowed to go home but retained his commission with the understanding that he could be called back into service.

In June 1780, Weedon was ordered to return to active service.[232] He served around his hometown of Fredericksburg, gathering recruits to be sent to Chesterfield Courthouse. During Leslie's Raid, Weedon was ordered to come immediately to Richmond to assist General Muhlenberg in organizing the defenses along the James River.[233] In February 1781, after Weedon had commanded militia at different times, Steuben suggested that Weedon return to command the Virginia Continentals over Muhlenberg or Scott (who was still a prisoner of war). Thirteen field officers including Richard Campbell, William Davies, Thomas Posey and Thomas Gaskins objected to Weedon returning to Continental service.[234] Eight reasons were given by the field officers, the main point of contention being that Weedon had left his command in 1778 and remained at home while other officers served faithfully in the field.[235] Despite the opposition of the officers, Steuben still brought Weedon back into command, but he placed him in charge of militia rather than Continental troops.

## Battle of Blandford

Starting in March, counties began to draft militiamen for eighteen months in Continental service. Steuben did not see a rush to arms from the populace. This was, in part, due to counties having portions of their militia in the field; by state law, they were not required to implement the law if they had militia already in the field. By the end of March, only seventy recruits had been brought into Chesterfield Courthouse.[236] On April 21, 1781, Steuben reported to Governor Jefferson that he had only 150 soldiers at Chesterfield who could be armed and scarcely enough officers to command them.[237] Steuben had intended to avoid sending these recruits into battle yet, but necessity overtook his preferences. In mid-March, 2,500 reinforcements were brought in with General William Phillips, who, after an expedition to Williamsburg, recrossed the James River to advance on Petersburg. General Muhlenberg rallied militia at Blandford, a village just outside of Petersburg, to resist the raid.

British General William Phillips. *National Archives.*

In the past studies of the battle, the accounts of the Battle of Blandford on April 25, 1781, mention that the only forces to engage the British on the field were militia from the surrounding counties, who had been hastily trained in Steuben's tactics. General Muhlenberg arranged the Virginians into two lines, with one regiment as a reserve along the Pocahontas Bridge in his rear and another regiment on the north bank of the Appomattox to watch and report if the British crossed the river to attack from that direction. After repeated attacks on the American lines, Muhlenberg was able to extract his force across the Pocahontas Bridge. The battle ended with an artillery duel between the two sides before Generals Muhlenberg and Steuben ordered the remaining troops to retreat toward Chesterfield.

Pension accounts, however, indicate that some of the Continentals from Chesterfield were sent to Blandford to assist Muhlenberg, led by Captains Joseph Scott, William L. Lovely and John Overton.[238] The Continentals, based on the pension application of veteran George Connolly, most likely fought on the second line of battle alongside Lieutenant Run. The Virginia Continentals, though a small portion of Muhlenberg's command, were active participants in the battle. Private Abner Gordon had only just fought at Guilford Courthouse a month prior and had been marched back to Virginia with baggage to Chesterfield, where he fell under the command of Captain Overton. Gordon later remarked that "after a slight skirmish with the British in passing over the Apommatox [Appomattox River] this declarant with the troops under the command of Baron Steuben retreated towards Richmond."[239] Private Jeremiah Haden, who had been marching from Fredericksburg with Captain Lovely, was wounded in the battle but was likely less seriously wounded, as he continued with the American retreat to Chesterfield and, later, Richmond.[240] Private George Connolly of Lovely's command offered the best description of the actions of the Virginia Continentals at Blandford in his pension declaration:

> *The Enemy appeared across the creek opposite of them and commenced firing upon our Army which had found access then along the street upon the opposite side of the creek after firing 23 rounds himself* [Connolly] *fell wounded both in his arm and his leg, the scars are now upon him. Our Army were compelled to retreat leaving him and John Johnson and about 18 others prisoners.*[241]

The next day, General Phillips crossed the Appomattox River and continued to march toward Richmond, though he stopped at Chesterfield

Courthouse to destroy the barracks and warehouses there. The Virginia Continentals skirmished with Phillips' force on April 27 near Chesterfield Courthouse, which resulted in some of them being captured. Private William Garrand, just recently returned from the Southern Army, received a bayonet wound in the right hip and remained a prisoner for the next six months.[242]

The battle at Blandford, despite the loss of Chesterfield Courthouse, served a purpose. It bought time for the arrival of a new Continental general, the Marquis de Lafayette, and nine hundred Continental light infantrymen at Richmond. The presence of this force prevented the capture of Richmond for a second time, and the British forces retreated to Petersburg. The Virginia Continentals, however, left Lafayette with his light infantrymen and militia to fight Phillips, while they were sent to the Albemarle Barracks at Charlottesville to organize with other recruits into a new battalion.

## Formation of Gaskins' Battalion

By mid-May, General Steuben had begun to gather and organize Continental recruits at Albemarle Old Courthouse, located about two miles west of present-day Scottsville. The number of recruits had increased to 430 officers and men by the end of the month, although most recruits were, as Steuben described them, "unarmed, unequip'd, and without cloaths."[243] To complete the battalion, Steuben reported that he needed 523 half shirts, 491 shirts, 311 overalls, 596 pairs of shoes, 499 hats and 299 blankets.[244] In addition, the battalion needed tents, camp kettles, axes, hatchets, knapsacks, haversacks and wagons with drivers to carry the supplies. Steuben also ordered 1,000 wooden canteens from the state.[245] Clothing was incoming from other places, and 1,100 new French muskets were en route to Albemarle Old Courthouse. Steuben had the men divided into eight companies, to recognize the eight Virginia Continental regiments that existed on paper. Lieutenant Colonel Thomas Gaskins of the Third Virginia was appointed commander of the new battalion, with Major John Poulson of the Eighth Virginia as his second-in-command.[246] On the evening of May 27, Lieutenant Henry Bedinger noted that shoes, shirts, hunting shirts, overalls and hats had arrived, though not enough for the entire battalion. The new clothing was issued to those who were most in need of clothing and footwear.[247] The arms arrived the same day, and once all the men were armed and some clothed in the new hunting shirts, Gaskins and his battalion were marched out to Point of Fork, the new arsenal established at the confluence of the Rivanna and James Rivers.

An ominous sign of future campaigns and conditions was that the battalion marched out amid "a heavy rain shower and hard claps of thunder," as Lieutenant Bedinger remarked in his journal. Bedinger also remarked on the condition of the officers:

> *Sometime previous to the March the Officers were ordered to draw espontoons and those who had not swords were obliged to draw large brass hilted unwieldy, very weighty ones, perhaps t'was meant as a stigma on those who had not provided themselves with neat ones.*[248]

Point of Fork was the property owned by David Ross, a Scotsman who was the commercial agent for Virginia in 1781. One of the wealthiest men in Virginia, Ross offered the peninsula that was set between the Rivanna and James Rivers to operate as an arsenal for Continental and state forces. Many of the military supplies from Richmond and Chesterfield had been relocated to Point of Fork, located roughly forty miles west of Richmond. The military situation had changed in Virginia by late May, and General Steuben became concerned for Point of Fork. Following the death of General Phillips at Petersburg on May 11, General Arnold assumed command of British forces in Virginia. This was short-lived, as General Cornwallis soon arrived with reinforcements. After resupplying at Wilmington, Cornwallis turned north and left South Carolina to be protected by British troops stationed across the state to threaten the supply lifeline of the Southern Army, Virginia.

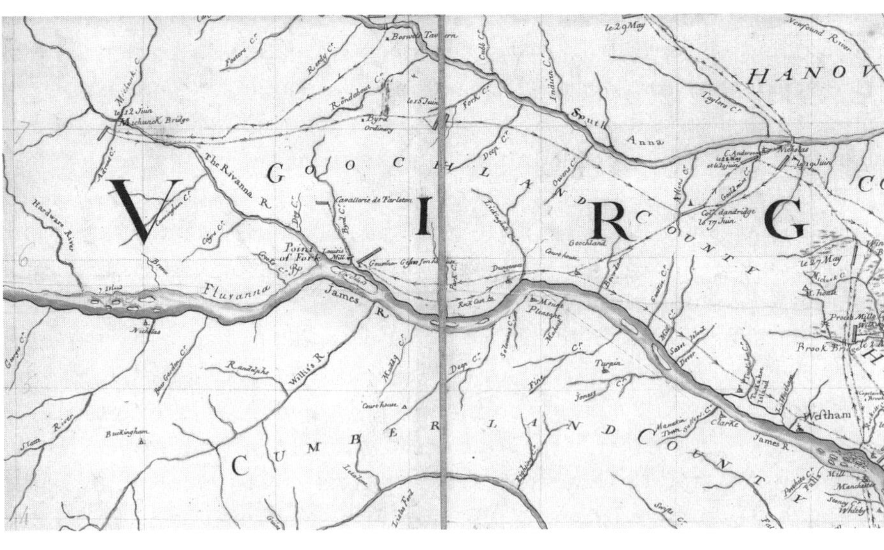

*Opposite*: Point of Fork map, 1781. *Capitaine Du Chesnoy, Michel, and Marie Joseph Paul Yves Roch Gilbert Du Motier Lafayette. Library of Congress.*

*Left*: Gaskins' Virginia Battalion, circa 1781. *Courtesy of Don Troiani.*

"Washington, Steuben, De Kalb, Pulaski, Kosciuszko, Lafayette, Muhlenberg." *Miriam and Ira D. Wallach Division of Art, Prints and Photographs: Print Collection, New York Public Library Digital Collections.*

Cornwallis also thought that Greene would possibly turn his forces to pursue him and prevent the possible loss of South Carolina. In a strange moment in the American Revolution, opposing armies marched in opposite directions, with Cornwallis on the march to Virginia and Greene on the march to South Carolina. Cornwallis' arrival in Virginia increased the British strength to over 5,000, in the face of Lafayette's roughly 2,100 men.[249]

In response, Genera Lafayette, who had assumed overall command from Steuben, elected to avoid battle with Cornwallis until he was able to gather more troops. In a move reminiscent of Greene's Race to the Dan three months earlier, Lafayette retreated from Richmond when General Cornwallis marched from Petersburg on May 24. As Cornwallis advanced against Lafayette, Lafayette simply marched in the opposite direction, intending to parallel Cornwallis' army rather than engage it. This bought time for more Virginia militia to report for service from northern and central Virginia, as well as riflemen from the Shenandoah Valley. Furthermore, this move closed the distance between Lafayette's army and the troops that had been ordered from Washington's Army. General Anthony Wayne was en route with nine hundred men of the Pennsylvania Line to add more veterans to Lafayette's army. This move, however, left the Point of Fork Arsenal open to attack with few troops to defend it, except for a company of the State Garrison Regiment.

Steuben, no longer in overall command and able to focus on recruiting and sending reinforcements south, determined that the arsenal must be defended. Steuben ordered Gaskins' Battalion to march to Point of Fork; it was joined there by 300 Virginia militiamen led by General Robert Lawson. More Virginia Continentals were marched to this location from Carter's Ferry (present-day Cartersville) and Powhatan Courthouse, which brought the size of Gaskins' Battalion to 550 officers and men.[250] In addition to some Continental dragoons, Steuben's force at Point of Fork numbered around 900. Steuben planned to remain at Point of Fork only until the British threat had lessened. General Greene had written for Steuben to join him with Gaskins' Battalion and any other Continental forces he could bring.[251] This order, however, was written before Cornwallis appeared in Virginia, and so Greene canceled that order and told Steuben to remain in Virginia. This message was intercepted by the British, and for the time being, Steuben intended to leave Virginia with Gaskins' Battalion.

Cornwallis' overall plan was to move Lafayette away from Richmond and use his light forces to "destroy any magazines and stores in the neighbourhood which may have been collected either for his use or for General Greene's army."[252] Lafayette suspected that the target was the Hunter's foundry and arms manufactory at Fredericksburg, so he mirrored Cornwallis' suspected movements toward Fredericksburg. Though Cornwallis had some interest in taking Fredericksburg, there was a larger prize to the west. Governor Jefferson and the General Assembly had convened in Charlottesville, and then there were the military supplies at Point of Fork. Determining that these targets were of more importance and that he could not prevent the meeting of Wayne and Lafayette, Cornwallis turned his focus toward Charlottesville and Point of Fork.

## Point of Fork Raid

On June 1, Cornwallis sent two raiding forces ahead of his own army with different targets. Lieutenant Colonel Banastre Tarleton was sent to take Charlottesville, disrupt the General Assembly and possibly capture Governor Jefferson. This plan was, in part, thwarted by the early warning of John Jouett to Jefferson and the assembly. Several members of the assembly were captured after militia and state troops failed to prevent the crossing of Tarleton's forces along the Rivanna River.[253] Tarleton was successful in burning supply wagons in Louisa County carrying clothing for the Southern Army, along with one thousand "new firelocks that had been manufactured at Fredericksburg" that were broken by Tarleton's men, and he destroyed four hundred barrels of gunpowder, several hogsheads of tobacco and some clothing and accouterments for the Continental Army.[254] While Tarleton raided Charlottesville and Cornwallis followed, Lieutenant Colonel John Graves Simcoe led the second raiding force toward Point of Fork.

Lieutenant Colonel Simcoe commanded the Queen's Rangers, a loyalist unit that consisted at the time of 200 infantrymen and 100 cavalrymen fit for service. Simcoe's force was augmented by 200 men from the Seventy-First Regiment, Hessian Jägers and a three-pounder.[255] Cornwallis' initial report showed that only 450 Continentals were stationed at Point of Fork, so Simcoe's 500-man force was seen as able enough for the job. They left the same day as Tarleton and advanced southward through Louisa and Fluvanna Counties after crossing over the South Anna River. As Simcoe neared Napier's Ford on the Rivanna River (near modern-day Palmyra), he learned from prisoners there that his advance was unknown to Steuben.[256] Simcoe also learned that Steuben's force was roughly twice what had been reported. Simcoe, regardless of this fact, decided to proceed cautiously

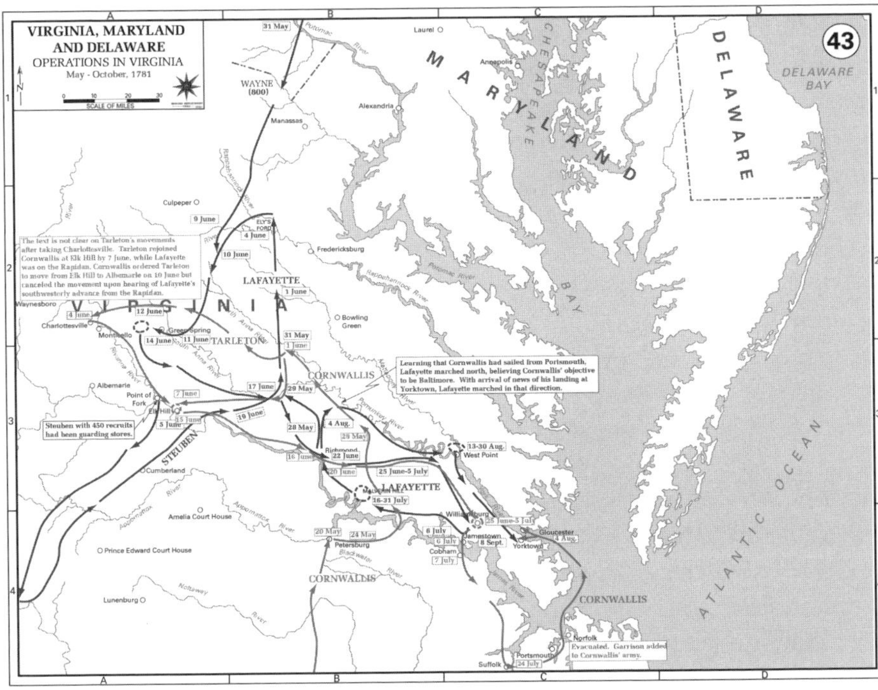


Map of Virginia operations, 1781. *Courtesy of the United States Military Academy Department of History.*

to Point of Fork. Simcoe's arrival at Napier's Ford, however, was quickly discovered after an interaction between Simcoe's scouts and some militiamen at the home of Colonel John Thompson. Two militiamen were captured at Napier's Ford, and Simcoe learned from them that Steuben had indeed found out about Simcoe's advance on June 3.

Steuben received a report from a Continental dragoon that not only was Simcoe's force advancing from the west, but Cornwallis' army was also marching directly through Goochland to the east. Even with his men armed, Steuben did not believe that his force could face Simcoe's, let alone two forces advancing from two directions. Retreat was the only reasonable option. Gaskins' Battalion, though armed, lacked almost any cartridge boxes, and the few they had were slung over the shoulder by rope.[257] Some of the men also received the new linen short jackets that were trimmed in blue but lacked many other articles of clothing. Steuben feared that his men would desert because of their condition. "The soldier who would gladly sacrifice his life in a battle for his country before the enemy," Steuben wrote to Archibald Cary, "revolted to see himself seized with misery for want of clothing."[258] Steuben believed it was absurd to make a stand with troops in such a terrible condition.

Steuben moved his force to the south side of the James River on the morning of June 5, after trying to transfer supplies across the river the day before. By the time Simcoe arrived in the vicinity of the American camp, most of the American force was across the James. Simcoe made an immediate attack with his cavalry against the picket guard protecting the last boats along the banks of the James.[259] Thirty men were captured by the cavalrymen, including several men of Gaskins' Battalion.[260] Some of the Americans continued to fire from across the James toward Simcoe's men, though with very little effect. Private James Slaton recalled the skirmishing between the two sides in his pension declaration in 1832:

> *Very shortly after we crossed the River we discovered the British troops entering the Town we had just left. The British fired one field Piece at our army and killed a mare from under officer, who he believes was a Captain—our troops were marched on the opposite side of a hill from which place men were dispatched to sink the boats in order to prevent the British from crossing in pursuit, in which party, he the said Slaton went, and assisted in sinking the boats.*[261]

It is noted that most of the men along the river fled at the shot of the three-pounder from the British and that after "much persuasion and threats," the men returned to their post.[262] Steuben also sent men up to five miles in either direction along the river to ensure that there were no large boats to allow Simcoe or Cornwallis to pursue him. That night, Steuben began to withdraw his forces with the intention of marching to join General Greene. To convince Simcoe that his force was still on the high ground overlooking the river, he left an officer and a company of Continentals to keep up fires using many fence rails that the men had gathered throughout the day.[263] Steuben marched south toward Cumberland Courthouse and then to Charlotte Courthouse, where Lawson's militia were left. While on the march, Steuben came across a supply of shirts meant for the Maryland troops in Greene's Army. Steuben either requested from the wagon driver, John Randall, the shirts for his men or forcefully took them, but regardless of the method, he solved one issue to his clothing conundrum.[264] Gaskins' Battalion marched as far south as Cole's Ferry on the Staunton River. Over the course of five days, sixty men had deserted from Gaskins' Battalion; twenty-four deserted from Captain Lovely's Company alone.[265] Steuben decided to halt here and rest the men after five days of hard marching. While he rested, Steuben used the time to indulge himself in a new delicacy he discovered in Virginia: black snakes. Men of Gaskins' Battalion were sent out by Steuben to hunt down black snakes or, as Steuben referred to them, "bush eels."[266]

Government officials disputed whether Steuben succeeded or failed at Point of Fork. In terms of goods lost or captured, Simcoe reported he destroyed 2,500 muskets, a large quantity of gunpowder and cannon shot, sixty hogsheads of rum and brandy, several chests of carpenters' tools, upward of four hundred entrenching tools, casks of flints, sailcloth and other supplies.[267] The largest loss seemed to be ten French artillery pieces, which were abandoned and later returned to American service.[268] Despite the loss of the supplies, Steuben was able to preserve Gaskins' Battalion, and the site itself was in operation, producing war materials, within a month of the raid. While encamped at Cole's Ferry, Steuben received his orders from Greene to remain in Virginia and report to Lafayette's command. Gaskins' Battalion joined Lafayette's army in Hanover County on June 19.

## Hobkirk's Hill

While Steuben and Gaskins' Battalion marched around Virginia, the Virginia Brigade marched into South Carolina. Despite the brigade receiving new coats around the time of Guilford Courthouse, it still suffered in terms of clothing. Lieutenant Colonel Richard Campbell wrote to Governor Jefferson on April 3 while encamped along the Deep River in North Carolina:

> *When I martched from the State of Virga. to join the Army I received a Pare of Overalls for Each Soldier, made of Ozenbrigs which did not last them more than two or three Weeks, and also a shirt for Each Soldier which are intirely worn out and them distresed for every kind of Cloathing Except Coats. I have obtained leave of Genl. Greene to send an officer to the state of Virginia, in order to procure such Cloathing as the men stand most in kneed of and Capt. Edmonds is the officer appointed for that business, who will hand you this.*[269]

The Virginia Brigade marched into South Carolina and encamped near Camden on April 19. Around the same time, a new light infantry company was formed from the ranks of the Virginia Brigade. The company was led by Captain Simon Morgan. A second light infantry company was led by Lieutenant Reuben Long. A veteran of five years, Long had experience in

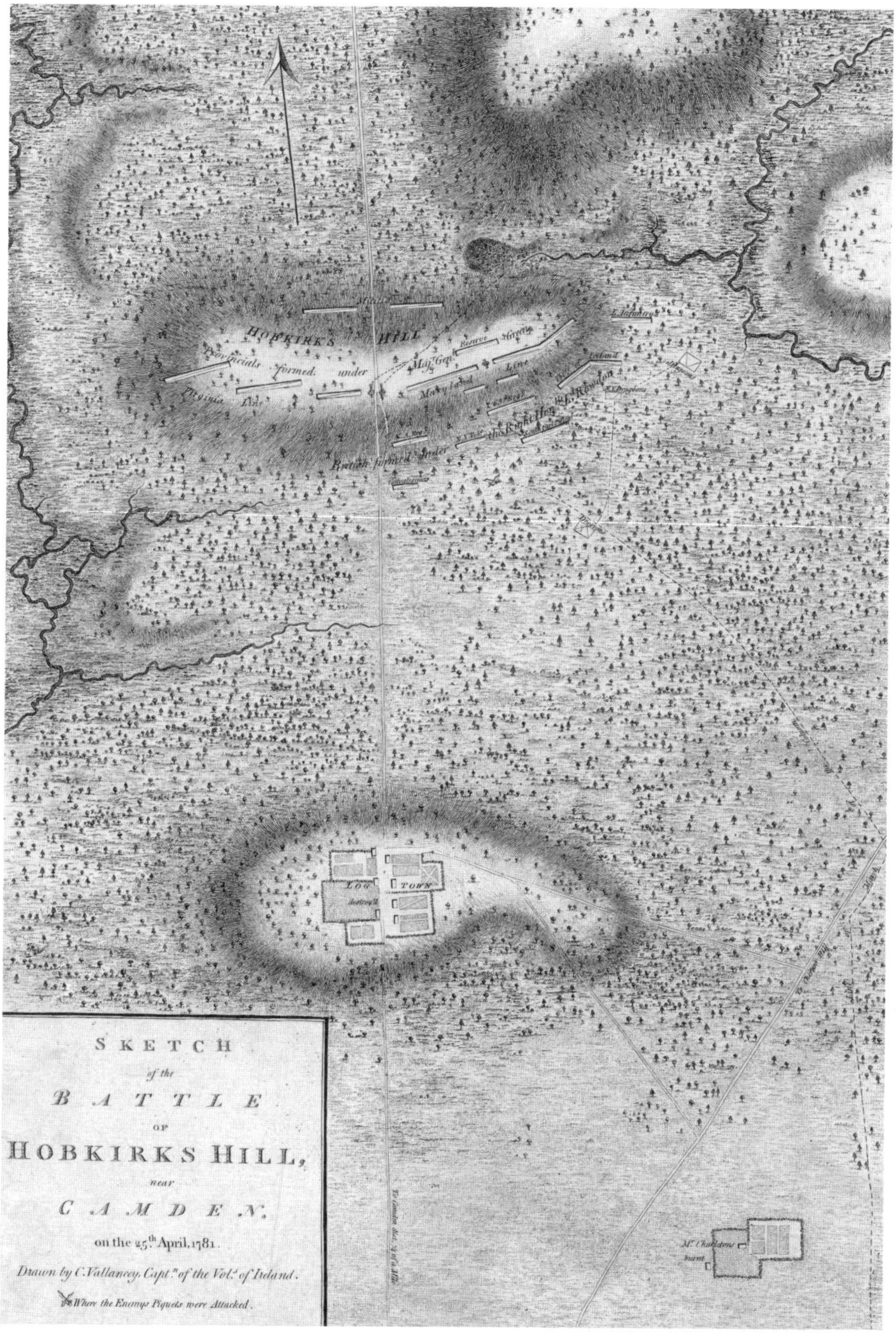


"Sketch of the battle of Hobkirks Hill, near Camden, on the 25th April, 1781." *Lionel Pincus and Princess Firyal Map Division, New York Public Library. New York Public Library Digital Collections.*

light infantry fighting, having served in Rawling's Virginia and Maryland Rifle Battalion in 1776 and then in the Morgan's Rifle Regiment during the Saratoga Campaign.[270] Reuben had assumed command of Andrew Wallace's company in October 1780 and had commanded it under Colonel Hawes at Guilford Courthouse before he was selected to command a company of light infantry to operate with Colonel William Washington and his cavalry command.[271] Other Virginians were temporarily transferred to the light infantry of Lee's Legion as he was sent to operate with Francis Marion's South Carolina troops against British outposts.[272] The Virginians in Lee's Legion were present at the successful siege of Watson, which surrendered on April 23.

While Colonel Lee besieged Fort Watson, General Greene provoked battle near Camden. Greene found a larger force at Camden than he expected and stronger fortifications as well. The garrison was commanded by Lord Francis Rawdon, and his force consisted mostly of American Provincials and Loyalist militia. With 1,250 men, Greene was determined to draw Rawdon into a battle rather than assault the fortified position. Private Robert Tait of the First Virginia recalled a skirmish that took place on April 22:

> *A party of British and Torys had entrenched near some mills. Col. Campbell obtained leave to take a party of men and route them—this he did so effectively that he nearly destroyed the whole of them.*[273]

Sergeant Major William Seymour of the Delaware Company reported on the same skirmish in his journal:

> *The same day happened a skirmish between a detachment of Colonel Campbell's Regiment and a picquet of the enemy's at a mill near Campden, in which the enemy were obliged to abandon their post. Of our men were slightly wounded one Lieutenant and one private. Of the enemy were four killed and five wounded.*[274]

Private John Carson also went with Captain Morgan's Light Infantry to probe the British positions:

> *After various skirmishing for something like eight or ten days, we crossed the Catawba and took our position on the south side of the Town and here he was in a skirmish at a redoubt under the command of Capt. Morgan. After remaining a short* [time] *at this position we were marched back to our old Camp ground.*[275]

*This page*: Morgan's light infantrymen skirmished around redoubts like this one outside of Camden. *Author's collection.*

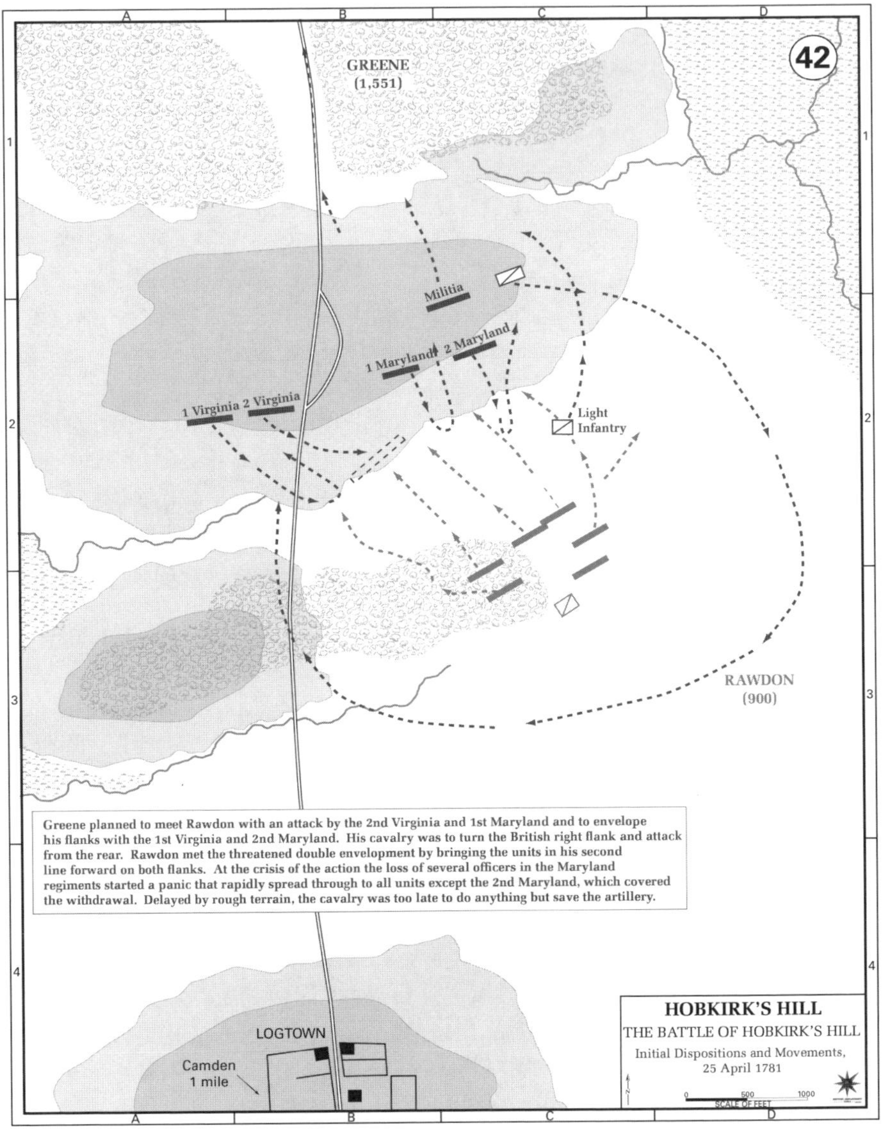


Battle of Hobkirk's Hill battle map. *Courtesy of the United States Military Academy Department of History.*

On April 25, the same day that Virginia Continentals fought in the Battle of Blandford, the Virginia Brigade engaged in battle at Hobkirk's Hill, roughly two miles north of Camden. Lord Rawdon marched with 900 men to engage Greene's Southern Army. General Huger was placed with his Virginia Brigade on the right side of Waxhaws Road, with Colonel Otho Williams' Maryland Brigade positioned on the left side. Three six-pounders were placed in the center on the road, with Morgan's Light Infantry and Kirkwood Delaware Continentals in front and a battalion of North Carolina Militia and Colonel Washington's cavalry in reserve. On the morning of April 25, the First Virginia Regiment (led by Lieutenant Colonel Campbell) constituted the right wing of the Virginia Brigade with 273 officers and men. The Second Virginia (led by Lieutenant Colonel Hawes) constituted the left wing of the Virginia Brigade with 359 officers and men. This brought the brigade strength at Hobkirk's Hill to 632 officers and men.[276]

Rawdon led his force by a circuitous route to attack Greene's left flank. His flank march caught the Americans off guard: many of the troops were in the creek behind the lines washing their clothes.[277] The advanced pickets from Captain Morgan's company were the first to detect the enemy's movements and spread the alarm. While the majority of Greene's Army quickly got into formations, Morgan's men, along with a company of Maryland Continentals and the Delaware Continentals, delayed Rawdon's force. Greene observed that the British line was shorter than his own and decided to attack Rawdon's line. The Second Maryland Regiment was ordered to attack Rawdon's right flank, and the First Virginia Regiment was ordered to attack the left. The First Maryland Regiment and the Second Virginia Regiment were ordered to attack in front with support from the artillery.[278] Rawdon extended his flanks with his reserves, and the battle became general along the entire line. In the battle, the Virginians fought principally against American Loyalist Provincials. The First Virginia went against the New York Volunteers, while the Second Virginia went against the King's American Regiment.

The battle seemed to be going well for the Americans, especially on the right flank, where Huger's Virginians not only stopped any attacks but actually gained ground against the Loyalist troops in their front. The tide, however, would change due to confusion. The two right companies of the Second Maryland became disorganized, and Colonel John Gunby ordered four of his companies to halt the advance and reform with the other two companies once he organized them. The order was misunderstood, and the entire Second Maryland fell back, which in turn caused the First Maryland to do the same.[279] Lieutenant Colonel Campbell was slightly wounded, and his own First Virginia became disorganized in the attack when they wheeled their line under fire from the enemy, so he was forced to halt his advance to redress the line.[280] The only regiment that was not halted in the advance by confusion was Lieutenant Colonel Hawes' Second Virginia. Hawes advanced to within fifty yards of the British line and stood the fire before Greene personally ordered them to withdraw. The First Virginia had rallied but did not advance and left the Second Virginia to enfilade fire from the New York Volunteers on their right. Hawes rallied on Campbell's Virginians, as well as the North Carolina Militia led by Colonel James Read, and attempted to stop the British advance. Lieutenant Colonel Guilford Dudley of Read's North Carolina Battalion wrote that in that moment, the battle line was "an universal blaze of musketry from left to right" and that every American officer exhorted "all the bravery and energy of his soul."[281]

Eventually, Greene was forced to withdraw his forces off the field. The Virginia Brigade, despite the confusion in the First Virginia, appeared to have held themselves well against Rawdon's forces. Private Edward Moody of the First Virginia claimed to have fired twenty-two rounds before the First Virginia left the battlefield.[282] The brigade had 15 killed, 63 wounded and 37 missing, for a total of 115, or 18 percent of the brigade's total strength. The Second Virginia suffered the most as they were outflanked by the withdrawal of the First Virginia and so lost 22 percent of their strength. In addition to this, Captain Morgan's company suffered heavily in the battle: he reported out of the 50 officers and men that went into battle, 10 were wounded and 8 were missing. Many of the missing, however, returned to the ranks at Sand Creek eight miles away due to a misunderstanding of orders regarding where to rally after the battle.[283] Private Isaac Stephens of the Second Virginia witnessed the death of his brother Peter during the battle.[284] Private John Fryer of the First Virginia recalled after the war that he lost all but one of his messmates, and the remaining messmate was severely wounded.[285] Private James Lewis of the Second Virginia received head wounds from a British dragoon during the battle, which he complained he had not recovered from in 1818 when he applied for his pension.[286] Greene overall had 271 Americans killed, wounded or missing.

Greene remained around Camden following the battle at Hobkirk's Hill. He had not yet lost his spirit to take South Carolina, declaring in a letter to his friend the Chevalier de La Luzerne, "We fight, get beat, rise and fight again."[287] Greene himself congratulated the men on their actions at Hobkirk's Hill, especially the light infantry of Morgan and Kirkwood, but stated with regret, "Our loss is so considerable that it is only to be lamented that the troops were not unanimous of the disposition to embrace so excellent an opportunity of gaining a victory."[288] Greene still had hopes to engage Rawdon and assault the weakened fortified positions at Camden. Despite his victory, Rawdon had lost 262 men, or roughly 30 percent, and with Cornwallis on the march to Virginia, he was left in overall command in South Carolina. On May 7, 500 Loyalist militia arrived to reinforce Rawdon's position, which forced Greene to move farther away to avoid a surprise attack from Rawdon. Rawdon did march from Camden the next day to trick Greene into battle but was unsuccessful, and on May 9, he abandoned Camden. This prompted Greene to send detachments led by Marion, Lee and Thomas Sumter to attack different outposts in the interior of South Carolina, while Greene himself took Camden and then turned west toward the town of Ninety-Six. The hope was to keep the British off balance while they threatened all the outposts at once and force the British to withdraw to the coast and thus surrender the majority of South Carolina.

In the aftermath of Hobkirk's Hill, General Greene set to restoring the discipline of his troops. During this time, the Virginia Brigade saw the court martial and punishment of men from their own unit. On April 30, five deserters were found guilty of desertion, joining the British army and bearing arms against the United States. One of these deserters was Private William Hennelly of the First Virginia, who was captured with the others around Camden either before or at the Battle of Hobkirk's Hill.[289] Hennelly, alongside the other four deserters from Maryland, Delaware and South Carolina, was hanged before the troops on May 1. The following day, another court martial was held for Ensign John Spitzfathom of the First Virginia:

> *Ensign Spitzfathom of the Virginia Line was charged by Lieutenant Colonel Campbell, with sleeping on Guard and suffering Capt. Armstrong to take him and all the guard Prisoners without discovering of him. Also with suffering part of his Guard to go into the Country a plundering and continuing till the night before they returned.*[290]

Spitzfathom was found guilty of only the first charge and was cashiered. On May 13, another soldier of the Virginia Line was brought up on desertion. Private John Blackburn, who had served with Colonel Buford, was charged with desertion, joining the enemy and bearing arms against the United States. Blackburn pled guilty to desertion but not guilty to the other charges. The charge of desertion was enough to warrant a death sentence, and he was hanged before the entire army on May 19.[291]

## The Siege of Ninety-Six

The Ninety-Six settlement was the westernmost outpost established by the British in South Carolina in 1780, and General Greene saw it as the last major British outpost besides Camden. With Camden under American control and the forces of Andrew Pickens, Henry Lee and Francis Marion engaging the smaller outposts, Greene turned his attention to Ninety-Six. Greene arrived with his army on May 22. Defending the fortified town was Lieutenant Colonel John Cruger with 550 Loyalist Provincials from New Jersey, New York and South Carolina. Defying traditional siege tactics, Greene did not send an immediate call for surrender to Cruger and began to dig his first lines seventy yards from Cruger's position. Attacks from Cruger's men quickly convinced Greene to open the lines farther away.

General Huger was still in command of the Virginia Brigade at Ninety-Six but was assigned by Greene to run operations in the camp. The command of the front lines was assigned to Lieutenant Colonel Campbell, who still retained command of the First Virginia. Command was changed in the Second Virginia Regiment as Lieutenant Colonel Hawes left the army due to illness, and his second-in-command, Major Thomas Ridley, also left the army. In the arrangement of officers that took place at Chesterfield Courthouse in February 1781, Major Ridley had been declared a supernumerary officer without a command, but because of the proximity of battle at Guilford and at the request of General Greene, Major Ridley, as well as Major Thomas Hill of the First Virginia, remained in the field until other officers could arrive. Major Smith Snead arrived in camp around Ninety-Six in May and replaced Major Ridley as commander of the Second Virginia Regiment.[292] Major Hill remained with the First Virginia until after the Siege of Ninety-Six, when he retired from service.

The service of the Virginians at Ninety-Six consisted of digging trenches against the Loyalist positions, particularly the eight-pointed star fort that commanded the ground around Ninety-Six. The men were broken into detachments to allow for rest and provide protection as they dug into the South Carolina clay under the hot sun. Cruger and his Loyalists did not allow them much rest, for as Sergeant David Wegar of the First Virginia recalled, the Americans "were attacked by the British forces almost every night, and sometimes twice of a night."[293] Private Bartholomew Cyrus of the Second Virginia described the experience of the Virginia Continentals at Ninety-Six best in a letter to support his pension application in 1821:

The American trenches that the Virginians helped build at Ninety-Six. *Author's collection.*

View of Star Fort from the Second Parallel. *Author's collection.*

> *We lay at ninety six siege near 1 month scarcely 1 hour in the night but firing like claps of thunder many days we could not get any thing to eat 40$ was cried through the camp for 1 hoecake of bread and it could not be got we were like hogs that had been wallowing when we came out of the intrenchment.*[294]

Eventually, Greene had moved his trenches close enough to storm the fortifications, and with the reinforcement of Lee's Legion and Andrew Picken's South Carolina Militia, Greene decided to attack. A report also came in that two thousand troops from Charleston were en route to reinforce Ninety-Six, so the pressure was placed on Greene to gain a victory. Colonel Lee was to lead his legion and some light infantry from the Virginia Brigade against the stockaded village, while Lieutenant Colonel Campbell was ordered to lead the attack with the First Maryland and First Virginia. A forward detachment of fifty men was chosen from the two regiments to spearhead the attack on the Star Fort, and some of the men carried long hooks to tear down the sandbags placed on top of the earthworks. The Maryland Continentals were led by Lieutenant Isaac Duval, and the Virginia Continentals were led by Lieutenant Samuel Selden of the First Virginia.

The attack took place on June 18. Colonel Lee's attack was successful after nearly an hour of heavy fighting. Private Edward Sims of Lieutenant Long's light infantry company was part of a detachment that led the attack of Lee's men. A sergeant and twelve men (including Sims) were sent ahead to clear abatis from the front to create a passage for the attack. Sims was badly wounded in the ankle and disabled for the remainder of his service. Of the sergeant and twelve men who were sent ahead, Sims reported, the sergeant and eleven of the men were killed or wounded in the attack.[295]

Star Fort at the Siege of Ninety-Six, South Carolina. *National Park Service.*

*Left*: View of the British stockade that the light infantry attacked on June 18. *Author's collection.*

*Below*: After taking the stockade, the light infantry turned toward the jail across the creek but did not take it. *Author's collection.*

From this position, the Forlorn Hope attacked the Star Fort on June 18. *Author's collection.*

Along the Star Fort, the forlorn hope led by Duval and Selden made it to the fortifications. As General Greene reported after the siege, "never was greater bravery exhibited" than by Duval's and Selden's men in their attack, but they struggled to breach the lines due to the height of the earthworks and the "galling fire" from the fort.[296] The attack on the Star Fort failed when two parties from within the fort exited and attacked the Americans from two sides. Vicious hand-to-hand combat took place as both Lieutenants Duval and Selden fell wounded. Greene believed that further attacks would only result in further losses and called off the attack of Campbell's men. The next day, with 2,000 troops led by Lord Rawdon bearing down on Ninety-Six, Greene lifted the siege and led his roughly 1,300 men northward.

General Greene reported 155 Americans killed, wounded or missing.[297] Captain William Bentley of the Second Virginia was captured during the siege, though the date is unknown. Besides Lieutenant Selden, Lieutenant William Evans was wounded for the third time in the war, and Lieutenant Thomas Miller was also wounded. The Virginia Brigade itself reported 41 killed, 36 wounded and 17 missing or captured, for a total of 94, or roughly 60 percent of the American casualties in the siege. Private Chapman Poindexter of the Second Virginia was wounded multiple times in the body and thighs and captured during the assault on the Star Fort.[298] Private Edward Moody of the First Virginia was also wounded at the Star Fort: he lost most of the fingers on his left hand to an officer's sword and received several blows to the head from the same. Thomas Purdom of the First Virginia was severely wounded by a bayonet through the body and was carried off the field and eventually to Charlotte, North Carolina, to heal.[299] Sergeant Edward Nunnelly of the First Virginia was one of the lucky survivors of the forlorn hope, though four musket balls passed through his coat, one grazing his arm.[300]

Although the Siege of Ninety-Six was unsuccessful, Greene's advance into South Carolina and attempt to take the outpost was a frightful reminder to British commanders that their forces were stretched thin across the state. After an unsuccessful pursuit of Greene, Rawdon rallied his forces at Ninety-Six but decided the outpost was too isolated. Despite the victory, Cruger had lost eighty-five men killed or wounded, and if Rawdon departed, there was little chance of reinforcements if a second siege took place. Rawdon also feared increasing numbers among South Carolina state forces and being so far from the security of the coast, and he decided it was not worth the effort to defend the town. By early July, Ninety-Six had been abandoned and burned, and many of the Virginia Continentals, like Privates Moody and Poindexter, who had been captured, were paroled and sent home to Virginia.[301]

General Greene attempted to pursue Rawdon's force, but due to the late arrival of South Carolina troops led by Sumter and Marion, Greene was unable to catch up. After spending the past two months marching over three hundred miles, Greene encamped his men on the High Hills of the Santee in South Carolina. While there, the men were issued rice bread, which, according to Lieutenant Colonel Lee, was despised by the Virginians and Marylanders, who had "grown up in the use of corn or wheat bread."[302] Meat was also a scarce resource for the men but was made up for in frogs and, occasionally, alligators.

Over the spring of 1781, the Virginia Continentals, both in the Carolinas and in Virginia, had engaged in several battles and skirmishes. Though nearly all these battles were defeats in some way, they proved that the Virginia Continentals were not out of the war and certainly were able to maintain themselves against the enemy, despite lack of supplies. This "fight, defeat and fight again" spirit was proven at Hobkirk's Hill, Blandford and Ninety-Six, but the deciding campaigns for the Revolution were only about to begin, and the Virginia Continentals would again find themselves on the field to prove their worth.

Chapter 6

# THE ROAD TO VICTORY

## SERVICE WITH "MAD ANTHONY"

While Gaskins' Battalion was encamped on the plantation of Colonel Dandridge, the commander of the battalion was changed. Colonel Christian Febiger, having spent the past nine months in Philadelphia forwarding supplies to Virginia, had returned to Virginia, and being senior to Gaskins, he assumed command of the battalion.[303] There was much debate over the matter, as Gaskins was intended to be the commander and Febiger was supposed to be organizing recruits in the place of Colonel William Davies, who had been appointed commissioner of war for the state. Febiger believed that he deserved the field command as the senior field officer in the state. Regardless of the argument, the battalion was commanded by Febiger for the next month. The Virginians marched east from Richmond in the direction of Bottom's Bridge, though they were in terrible condition, according to Colonel Febiger. On June 30, Febiger wrote to Colonel Davies about the condition of Gaskins' Battalion:

> *But Lord have mercy upon us, a modest army of Women on examining Any Thing lower than the navel, would instantly take to their Scrapers on the Appearance of so many naked Clubs.... The fact is the men are literally naked, shirts and Blanketts excepted.*[304]

While encamped on the peninsula, Lafayette also reorganized the Virginia troops to create a light infantry corps from the Virginia troops (militia, state troops and Continentals).[305] Some of Gaskins' men were detached to serve in the light infantry under Major John Wills, who was also a Continental officer.[306] Cornwallis marched his army to Williamsburg, occupying the town on June 25. Lafayette followed behind him, waiting for an opportunity to deal a blow against Cornwallis. Some of the Virginia light infantry fought in the Battle of Spencer's Ordinary near Williamsburg on June 26, including men from Major Willis' command, but no Virginia Continentals recalled being engaged in the battle. The men were encamped at New Kent Courthouse over the next week before they marched again in the direction of Williamsburg when Cornwallis withdrew from the town on July 4.

On the morning of July 6, General Anthony Wayne led an advanced guard consisting of Pennsylvania Continentals and Virginia light infantrymen and riflemen in the direction of Green Springs Plantation near Jamestown Island. They discovered the picket line of Cornwallis' army and indications that Cornwallis was crossing the James River. Wayne reported that Cornwallis had only a rear guard on the north side of the river, which caused Lafayette to order his light infantry and the remainder of the Pennsylvania Line to join Wayne at Green Spring. Colonel Gaskins' Battalion remained in position at Chickahominy Church, about eight miles away from the growing battle at Green Spring.[307]

Major Willis led his light infantry against the British pickets consisting of soldiers from the Seventy-Sixth and Eightieth Regiments. After roughly two hours of skirmishing, the British pickets were pushed back by the combined weight of Wayne's Pennsylvanians, with some of Lafayette's light infantry corps rallied on the Pennsylvanians' left flank. Major Willis, alongside the command of Major Elliott Rucker's militia, gathered his command on the right flank. As Wayne advanced with his nine hundred men (including the light infantry), Cornwallis launched his surprise attack, consisting of two thousand British and Hessian soldiers who had been hiding behind the rise. The signal for this attack was the capture of abandoned British artillery just in sight of the troops. By this time, Lafayette had learned of the trap, but it was too late to stop Wayne. Wayne intended to buy time and check the enemy's advance by ordering a bayonet charge. The charge stopped the British line for a moment, but once the Americans halted to fire, Cornwallis began to hit both flanks of Wayne's line. The Virginia light infantry under Major Willis were forced back, though Private Christian Peters (a Virginia militiamen with Willis' command) recalled that "he was on the right where there was but little danger but Gen'l. Waynes regular Troops suffered very much."[308] The Pennsylvanians held their position for five minutes against the British line before they were forced to break to the rear, abandoning two six-pounders to the enemy.

Though it is not mentioned in official reports, the men of Gaskins' Battalion were definitely involved in different parts of the battle. Those who were under Major Willis' command were pushed back, rallied and helped cover the retreat of the Pennsylvanians.[309] Sergeant Charles McMinnis received a flesh wound in his right thigh during the battle; he appears to be the only man from Gaskins' Battalion known to have been wounded in the battle.[310] Private James Slaton of Captain Lovely's Company wrote of the involvement of the remainder of Gaskins' Battalion in the closing action of the Battle of Green Spring:

> *The day of the Battle at James Town the troops with which said deponent was left were ordered to James Town to coopperate in the Battle but were too late in their movements and met the American troops on their retreat from said battle ground and...the two detachments retreated together some distance.*[311]

After the Battle of Green Spring, Colonel Febiger was removed to gather more recruits at Cumberland Old Courthouse, and Lieutenant Colonel Gaskins regained command of the battalion. Gaskins' Battalion was attached to General Wayne's Brigade and marched back to Malvern Hills, where they crossed the James River into Chesterfield County on July 13. This move was to counter the raid of Tarleton's command. Once the entire British force was across the James River after Green Spring, Cornwallis sent Tarleton on a four-hundred-mile raid into south-central Virginia. General Lafayette split his forces and sent Wayne with five hundred Pennsylvania Continentals, Gaskins' Battalion (now consisting of three hundred officers and men) and some Virginia riflemen to Goode's Bridge in Amelia County.[312] Once encamped at Goode's Bridge, there was the possibility that Gaskins' Battalion, alongside the Pennsylvanians, would either march south to join General Greene or be sent to guard the Potomac River, depending on Cornwallis' next movement.

The thought of being sent to South Carolina horrified the men of Gaskins' Battalion. General Wayne reported that the Virginians were "murmuring and discontent" as there was a want for every type of clothing and pay.[313] The sentiment was felt by both officers and enlisted men, and Wayne feared that the mutinous behavior of the Virginians would spread to the Pennsylvania troops, who were in a similar condition and had already mutinied seven months before. This crisis was averted when Wayne's force was ordered to return to Lafayette's army near Bottom's Bridge on August 1. By the evening of August 8, the Virginians were encamped near Bottom's Bridge, where an incident took place between an officer and his soldier.

Around nine o'clock at night on August 8, Private James Grant, a twenty-three-year-old Irish shoemaker from Loudoun County, entered the tent of his commanding officer, Captain Abraham Kirkpatrick, and shot the officer in the head. The shot hit near the left eye, and though it did not kill Kirkpatrick, it did blind him in that eye for the remainder of his life. Sergeant Robert Bradshaw apprehended Grant, who admitted to shooting Kirkpatrick on account of Kirkpatrick sleeping with Grant's wife. Grant was taken to Colonel Gaskins' tent, where they met Kirkpatrick and he asserted that "he and his wife had parted that morning." On August 12, after pleading guilty to shooting the officer and being found not guilty of mutiny, Grant was hanged in the presence of Gaskins' Battalion and the Pennsylvania troops.[314] Tensions only rose throughout the month of August between the Virginians and the Pennsylvanians.

General Lafayette's letters to General Washington indicate that the Virginians and the Pennsylvanians did not like each other in prior campaigns and that their negative mood toward each other was worse now than it had been before.[315] General Wayne felt that his Pennsylvania Continentals were not being used well in Virginia and wished to march south to join General Greene in exchange for the six hundred Maryland recruits who were about to be sent there from Maryland. The Virginia authorities, as well as the soldiers, were angered by Wayne taking from Virginia supply posts to clothe his troops; the Virginians felt it was the duty of the Pennsylvania state government to supply their own troops, as it was the duty of the General Assembly to supply Virginia troops. Wanye even asked Lafayette if he could detach Gaskin Battalion when he was again ordered across the James River in mid-August. This was denied because the order was canceled, and instead, Wayne marched his force to Westover Plantation to drill and await further orders.[316] He was ordered to instill discipline in the battalion, with the help of one hundred veteran soldiers who had just arrived in Virginia.[317]

After fourteen months of imprisonment, many officers and men of the Virginia Continental Line who were captured at Charleston were exchanged at Jamestown Island in July 1781. Many of the enlistments of the Virginia Continentals were expired, and those soldiers were discharged, but one hundred soldiers who were deemed fit for service were placed under Captain Alexander Parker and assigned to Colonel Gaskins'

Battalion.[318] The men who served under Captain Parker had enlisted for the duration of the war and were promised furloughs home "so soon as the Exigency of the Service would admit of it."[319] The men were attached to Gaskins' Battalion at Newcastle, Virginia, but Wayne had ordered them to remain there when he marched to Westover because they weren't armed. Lafayette ordered them to join the battalion in the hopes that the veterans might have a good effect on the new recruits.[320] Captain Parker's veterans did not join the battalion until August 31, by which time General Wayne's force had crossed the James River and encamped at Eber's Point in Surry County. Their stay there was not long, however, for they marched to Cobham, across the river from Jamestown. There, Gaskins' men caught sight of the three thousand French soldiers arriving to reinforce the Americans at Williamsburg. On September 3, the Virginians crossed on French boats to Jamestown, and they marched into Williamsburg the next day. The same day, the French fleet under the Count de Grasse defeated a British fleet in the Battle of the Capes. This victory prevented a resupply and the possible escape of General Cornwallis' army, then stationed along the banks of the York River at a small town called Yorktown.

## Battle of Eutaw Springs

While Gaskins' men were encamped around the old capitol of Williamsburg, the Virginia Brigade was on the road to one of the last major battles of the American Revolution. They spent roughly a month on the High Hills of the Santee near "James' old Field." This time was used to rest the men, as they had "suffered incredible hardships."[321] The men were ordered to pitch their tents and be sure to "preserve cleanliness in camp." The roll was to be taken four times every day, according to orders of July 17, 1781. From sunrise to eight o'clock in the morning, the soldiers participated in company drill, and the battalions engaged in battalion drills from five o'clock in the afternoon until sundown. Brigade drills took place occasionally.[322] This preserved the discipline (at least on the field) of the Virginia Brigade. Discipline was also maintained through court martials and punishments. On July 21, Private Martin Phifer of the First Virginia received one hundred lashes on the bare back for the charge of desertion.[323] Two officers of the Virginia Brigade were also placed on trial. On July 20, Lieutenants Philip Easton and David Williams, along with two officers of the Maryland Brigade, were charged with forcibly taking shoes

The Battle of Eutaw Springs. *Miriam and Ira D. Wallach Division of Art, Prints and Photographs: Print Collection, New York Public Library Digital Collections.*

from the quartermaster stores at Salisbury, North Carolina, the previous spring. The officers were found not guilty of forcibly taking the shoes but guilty of taking the shoes without proper authority; they stated that "they are of opinion that the situation in which their troops were and the precedents which had been set them justified them in so doing."[324] General Greene also commented on this trial in his orders for July 25, stating that the officers "acted with a view of promoting the service" but should go through proper channels in the future.

The command of the brigade also changed. General Huger left the army due to illness, so Lieutenant Colonel Richard Campbell assumed command of the Virginia Brigade while Captain Thomas Edmonds was ordered to take command of the First Virginia Regiment.[325] Major Snead retained command of the Second Virginia Regiment. On a field return dated July 26, 1781, Campbell's Brigade had a paper strength of 967 officers and men, but only 407 of them present and fit for duty.[326] Over one-quarter of the men were absent sick, and though the officer-to-men ratio had declined to 1:25 (from 1:31 before the Battle of Guilford Courthouse), there were only fifteen officers present to command sixteen companies that day.

General Greene estimated that there were 4,000 British regular troops and 400 cavalrymen in South Carolina, in addition to 1,000 Loyalist militia. Even with the addition of 500 South Carolina state troops and 1,500 to 2,000 South Carolina militia, General Greene fell short of the 10,000 men he estimated were needed to retake Charleston. He was determined to, instead, strike the British forces while they were outside of Charleston, weakening the defenses of Charleston for a possible attack. Even if Greene's attack drove the British back into the city, it would free the majority of South Carolina and allow him to deny them supplies from the countryside through smaller raiding forces. Located along the Congaree River at Orangeburg were 2,000 British and Loyalist troops under the command of Lieutenant Colonel Alexander Stewart. Lord Rawdon had left South Carolina due to illness and left Stewart in command of forces.

Summer rains had flooded the swamps and streams toward McCord's Ferry where Stewart encamped his force, so Greene's army marched north on August 24 before turning southeast toward Howell's Ferry.[327] Stewart was afraid of being surrounded by Greene and the South Carolina militia and being cut off from the supplies and reinforcements expected from Charleston. He withdrew his troops to Eutaw Springs on August 27 to place himself closer to reinforcements and supplies. Greene arrived at McCord's

The Battle of Eutaw Springs. *Miriam and Ira D. Wallach Division of Art, Prints and Photographs: Print Collection, New York Public Library Digital Collections.*

Ferry on September 2, where South Carolina state troops and militia led by Marion and Pickens joined him. By September 7, Greene's Southern Army, numbering around 2,200 men, was encamped seven miles northwest of Eutaw Springs and prepared to attack Stewart's camps there.

Around four o'clock in the morning on September 8, General Greene put his army on the move toward Eutaw Springs. The column was led by Lee's Legion and South Carolina state troops, followed by North Carolina and South Carolina militia; the North Carolina Brigade, led by General Jetho Sumner; the Virginia Brigade, led by Lieutenant Colonel Richard Campbell; and the Maryland Brigade, led by Colonel Otho Williams. The Continental dragoons, led by Colonel Washington, and the Delaware Battalion, led by Captain Kirkwood, brought up the rear of Greene's force. In addition to these troops, Greene brought a detachment of the First Continental Artillery (recruited mostly from Virginia); two three-pounders were attached to the militia contingent, while two six-pounders were attached to the Continentals. Two American deserters, however, warned Lieutenant Colonel Stewart of Greene's advance, and he sent a scouting force of 190 infantry and cavalry down the road northeast of his position. The advance units of both armies clashed about three miles from the camp, which resulted in the British force being led into an ambush sprung by Lieutenant Colonel Lee and forced the British to withdraw to camp. This proved too late for 300 British soldiers who were sent out foraging. They had left camp early in the morning under Stewart's orders (before it was known that Greene was on the move) and had taken a path off the main road to find sweet potatoes on a nearby plantation. The gunfire of the opening skirmish caught their attention, and they unintentionally revealed themselves to the Americans, resulting in their capture.[328]

Greene formed two lines, deployed in a similar style as at Guilford Courthouse, to attack the British camp. The front line consisted of the militia supported by two three-pounders on the main road. The second line was made up of Greene's Continentals. The Maryland Brigade formed the left of the line with roughly 400 officers and men, the North Carolina Brigade with roughly 350 officers and men on the right, and the Virginia Brigade with 350 officers and men was positioned in the center.[329] In the center of the Virginia Brigade, two six-pounders commanded by Captain William Brown were placed. In reserve were Colonel Washington's cavalry and Kirkwood's Delaware Continentals. With the loss of the foraging party, this placed roughly 1,700 British and Loyalist troops against Greene's 2,200.

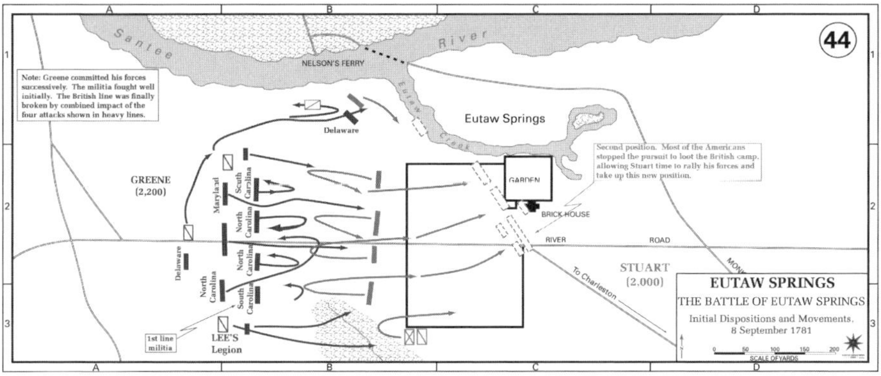


Map of the Battle of Eutaw Springs. Not noted are the Virginians in the center of the second American line. *Courtesy of the United States Military Academy Department of History.*

Artillery fire and the advance of the militia opened the attack on Stewart's position at nine o'clock in the morning. Supported on the flanks by South Carolina state troops and the infantry of Lee's Legion, the militia advanced within musket range and, in some cases, engaged in hand-to-hand combat with the British. Some of the militiamen fired up to seventeen rounds before they began to break to the rear. The North Carolina Continentals were sent in to bolster the line and, despite their relative inexperience in battle (many of them only enlisted in the past spring or summer), performed well as they attacked the British line, were repulsed and reformed to hold off another attack from the British.[330] Some prisoners were captured in the early portion of the attack, and these prisoners had an experience with the Virginia Brigade that left a lasting impression on the mind of Sergeant David Wegar of the Second Virginia:

> *There was a party of British soldiers which had been taken prisoners and were advancing in the direction where he was stationed; and the line to which he was attached supposing they were coming up for an attack—the American line fired on them, which caused great confusion for some time.*[331]

With the militia finally breaking under the weight of British musket and artillery fire and the North Carolina Continentals still heavily engaged alongside Lee's light infantry, General Greene turned toward his veterans of the Maryland and Virginia Brigades to carry on the battle and garner victory for the Americans. Colonel Otho Williams commanded the entire second line, and Greene's orders read, "Let Williams advance and sweep the field with his bayonets."[332] In the advance, Greene later reported, the Continentals "preserved their order and pressed on with such unshaken resolution that they bore down all before them."[333] Colonel Williams recalled the moment he gave the order for the charge:

> *Never was order obeyed with more alacrity. The two brigades received it with a shout. Emulous to wipe away the recollections of Hobkirk's Hill, they advanced with a spirit of the impatience with which they had hitherto been passive spectators of the action. When approached within forty yards of the enemy, the Virginians delivered a destructive fire, and the whole second line, with trailed arms and an animated pace, advanced to the charge. Until this period their progress had been in the midst of showers of grape, and under a stream of fire from the line opposed to them. But eye-witnesses have asserted that the roll of the drum and the shouts which followed it drew every eye upon them alone; and a momentary pause in the action, a suspension by mutual consent, appeared to withdraw both armies from a sense of personal danger to fix their attention upon this impending conflict.*[334]

It was during this charge that Lieutenant Colonel Campbell met his fate. As Lieutenant Colonel Lee rode up to Campbell, who was just behind the right flank of the First Virginia, Campbell was struck in the breast. He dropped forward in his saddle as he was led off by Private William Davis, who had been transferred from Campbell's command to serve in the cavalry of Lee's Legion.[335] His son, Lieutenant Archibald Campbell, was also present in the battle, and some accounts claim he was near his father when he was struck, though it is not clear if he went to the rear with his mortally wounded father or remained with the brigade for the remainder of the battle. Colonel Williams suggested in his recollections of the battle that Campbell's son remained with Campbell and actually held up his father as the Virginians charged forward.[336] Regardless, the Virginians continued forward under the hail of musket balls and grapeshot until they fired a volley at forty yards and charged into their foe. On the right side of the River Road, Captain Edmonds led his First Virginia against the New Jersey Loyalists, while Major Snead led the Second Virginia against the New York Loyalists and the Eighty-Fourth Regiment. It should be noted that the New Jersey and New York Loyalists were the same troops who had fought against the Virginians at the Siege of Ninety-Six. The infantry of Lee's Legion broke the British left and then wheeled to fire volleys down the ranks of the Sixty-Third Regiment, causing that regiment to break to the rear. Captain Edmonds' men broke the ranks of the New Jersey Loyalists, just as Snead's men did against the New Yorkers. The spirit of the Virginians and the Marylanders, possibly mixed with memories of Ninety-Six, meant they went into vicious hand-to-hand combat with their Loyalist opponents. Colonel Williams later remembered:

> *If the two lines on this occasion did not actually come to the mutual thrust of the bayonet, it must be acknowledged that no troops ever came nearer. They are said to have been so near that their bayonets clashed and the officers sprang at each other with their swords, before the enemy actually broke away.*[337]

In the midst of the mêlée, Lieutenant Robert Jouett of the First Virginia engaged in a personal battle against a British officer. Jouett fought with his sword while the British officer fought with a musket and bayonet. Both men dropped their weapons, and the two combatants turned to fists. While the men rolled on the ground, a British soldier tried to stab Jouett but only pierced his coat; the bayonet became entangled in the coat, bringing the soldier to the ground with them. The British soldier stood to attempt to stab Jouett again but was struck down by the sword of Lieutenant Edward Manning of Lee's Legion. Jouett then killed the officer with the butt of the British soldier's musket.[338]

The battle, from the point of view of the Americans, was turning into the great American victory of the South, with nearly the entire British force in disorderly retreat and abandoning their camps. Loyalist refugees, who had gathered in the camps in the days prior to the battle, fled down the road to Charleston, adding to the confusion.[339] The attack began to fall apart for two reasons. On the far right of the British line, British and Loyalist troops rallied in a stand of thickets and continued to fire into the American left flank, and Colonel Washington's cavalry failed to dislodge them from their position with a mounted charge, as did an attack by the Delaware Continentals. Farther past the British camp, the British were barricaded in a brick house and began to fire into the advancing Americans. Hungry and thirsty Continentals also paused in the British camp to loot food and other goods. These combined reasons led to a delay in the American advance and the reorganization of Stewart's troops. Greene's men, having used most of their ammunition and fought for four hours under the hot South Carolina sun, had had enough of fighting and began to withdraw over the body-strewn ground over which they had advanced. Some of the Virginians were nearly captured, including Private Tapley Lightfoot of the First Virginia, who had received two bayonet wounds in the arm and leg:

> *During the action this wing which was entirely composed of the two Virginia regiments above mentioned was over powered by superior numbers, and compelled to throw down their arms and ask for quarter. At this critical moment Colonel Washington arrived at the spot with his squadron of horse, made a furious charge upon the enemy's left then engaged with us and broke their line. Our two regiments resumed their arms, completed the defeat and came out of the action with him 360 prisoners.*[340]

Lightfoot most likely confused the cavalrymen of the South Carolina State Dragoons under Lieutenant Colonel William Henderson for Washington, as Colonel Washington had been wounded and captured by this point in the battle. Lightfoot and his comrades may have also been among the detachment led by Captain Edmonds as the Americans withdrew from the field. Sergeant Major Seymour of the Delaware Battalion described the withdrawal with Edmonds' Virginians:

> *Major Edmund with a small party of men joined our infantry in the British encampment, keeping up fire for a small space of time; found our army had withdrawn from field made it necessary for us likewise to withdraw. We brought off one of their three-pounders, which was with much difficulty performed through a thick wood for four miles, without the assistance of but one horse.*[341]

The remainder of the Virginia Brigade, now led by Major Snead, rallied only a short distance from the British camp and, after Greene established a strong picket from the South Carolina state troops, withdrew from the field. The Virginians arrived at their original encampment around two o'clock that afternoon.[342] Both sides claimed victory in the Battle of Eutaw Springs. Lieutenant Colonel Stewart saw the battle as a victory because he held his camps and captured two six-pounders from the Americans. Greene, however, had planned to fight the next day, but rain had prevented any further attacks. Stewart, however, had suffered heavily from Greene's attack, losing 882 of his roughly 2,000 officers and men (including the foragers captured early in the morning), which was nearly half his force. Stewart, after carrying away all but 70 wounded men and destroying many supplies, including 1,000 muskets, marched to Monck's Corner, roughly thirty miles from Charleston, on September 10. Greene pursued Stewart within twelve miles of Monck's Corner, where he halted because Stewart was now within close supporting distance of Charleston. Greene claimed victory because he considered Stewart to have given up the field and retreated to Charleston. Greene gave partial credit for his "victory" to the Continentals, including "free use of the Bayonet made by the Virginians and Marylanders."[343]

The greatest loss of the Virginia Brigade was Lieutenant Colonel Richard Campbell. Lieutenant Colonel Lee wrote that Campbell died after his orderly brought him to the rear and dismounted him during the fighting, but Lee's son, Confederate General Robert E. Lee, claimed that he survived for some hours and died shortly after being told that his men were victorious.[344] General Greene mentioned Campbell in his official report, describing him as "the great Soldier and the firm patriot.[345]

The Virginia Brigade went into battle with roughly 350 officers and men and lost 17 killed, 32 wounded and 4 missing for a total of 53, or roughly 15 percent of its strength. The overall American losses were 575 killed, wounded or missing, the South Carolina state troops and the militia having suffered heavier losses than the Continentals. It should be noted, however,

The Battle of Eutaw Springs. *Miriam and Ira D. Wallach Division of Art, Prints and Photographs: Print Collection, New York Public Library Digital Collections.*

that Lieutenant Colonel Lee later stated he believed that both Greene and Stewart had understated their losses in their reports. Besides the death of Lieutenant Colonel Campbell, the Virginia Line lost two more officers: Captain Conway Oldham (who had fought at the Battle of Cowpens) and Lieutenant John Wilson, who left behind two orphans in Virginia.[346] In addition, Captain Simon Morgan, who was noted for his actions at Hobkirk's Hill, was severely wounded in the hip and helped off the field by one of his sergeants.[347] Lieutenant Robert Jouett was also wounded in the battle, as well as Lieutenant Thomas Miller of Cowpens fame.

The wounds of the men provided evidence of the close-quarter fighting in which the Virginia Brigade was involved. Private Charels Clements of the First Virginia, having only recently returned to service after his Hobkirk's Hill wound, was shot through the left chest; the musket ball passed through his ribs, exited through his side and passed through his left arm, leaving him with four wounds from only one shot.[348] Private Richard Joy of the same regiment received four wounds total: two musket balls through the right thigh and right shoulder, a wound in the left arm from a broadsword and a bayonet wound through the breast.[349] Private Robert Owls, who followed the wounded Captain Morgan into the battle, received his second wound of the war when a musket ball broke his left leg.[350] Private Gabriel Murphey was wounded by a pistol shot from a horseman, whom Murphey quickly killed.[351] Corporal Matthew Cummings was captured with ten other Virginians during the withdrawal and spent the next fourteen months as a prisoner of war.[352] Private William Johnson of the Second Virginia was wounded on the top of the head by a sword, bayoneted in the left arm and shot in the knee, hip and leg.[353]

After pursuing Stewart for a few days and skirmishing with some Loyalists (during which one of the men of the Second Virginia was captured), the Virginia Brigade returned to their old encampment on the High Hill of the Santee to recover from the campaign.[354] Major Smith Snead retained command of the brigade, which now had fewer than three hundred officers and men fit for duty. As for the men of the Virginia Brigade, they had fought in the final major battle in South Carolina. General Greene's Southern Army had regained most of the Carolinas, and though unable to take the cities of Charleston and Savannah, it was able to contain any further advances into the countryside. The attention of Virginians at home, however, turned from the hills and swamps of South Carolina to the banks of the York River in Virginia.

## The Siege of Yorktown

On September 8, while the Virginia Brigade was engaged in the bloody fighting at Eutaw Springs, General Lafayette gathered French and American forces at Williamsburg. General Muhlenberg was placed in command of the advanced corps, consisting of Gaskins' Battalion, a detachment of Virginia riflemen and detachments from the militia brigades of General Stevens and Lawson.[355] The camp of Gaskins' Battalion was set at Springfield, roughly three miles from Williamsburg—where, ironically, Virginia Continentals had camped during the first two years of the Revolution.[356] Gaskins' men were involved in some skirmishes along the roads leading toward Yorktown, but no casualties were reported.[357] On September 15, Lieutenant Colonel Gaskins formed his men for a review by General George Washington. Washington had marched with seven thousand American and French troops from New York to help trap Cornwallis at Yorktown and arrived at Williamsburg on September 14. Washington was not pleased with the appearance and condition of the Virginia troops. He noted that the soldiers were totally lacking clothing and only one-third of the battalion was truly fit for field service.

Gaskins' Battalion remained attached to General Wayne's Brigade, which was attached to the Second Division under General Steuben. The Virginians formed part of the right wing of Washington's Army, which Governor Thomas Nelson Jr. recognized as the position of honor during a siege. Though Nelson was in command of the Virginia Militia during the siege, he was still worried about the appearance of the Virginia Continentals. He pressured Colonel Davies to supply clothing to Gaskins' Battalion, writing, "As their Troops are to take the Right of the whole Army you will judge how necessary it is that they be enabled to make a decent if not a respectable Figure."[358] Colonel Davies complained that it was the fault of the officers for holding back clothing from the men for themselves, though no other accounts suggest this. Regardless of this, the men of Gaskins' Battalion remained in their ragged and naked condition as they took part in the Siege of Yorktown.

The battalion suffered from illness: over one-third of the men fell ill, including Lieutenant Colonel Gaskins himself. Of the twenty-two company-grade officers listed in Gaskins' Battalion, only five were present and fit; the remainder were listed as "present sick."[359] Officers from the Virginia State Artillery were temporarily attached to Gaskins' Battalion to help with the command.[360] This left roughly 300 officers and men to participate in the

House of Cornwallis's surrender, Yorktown, Virginia. *Detroit Photographic Co., 1902. Library of Congress.*

siege out of the 604 officers and men listed in the battalion. The battalion had barely enough arms for the men and was wanting in everything else, including clothing and bayonets.[361] The battalion marched toward Yorktown on September 28 and was joined by Gaskins four days later. The men spent the first days of the siege constructing material for the front lines, which included 32 saucissons, 320 pickets, 32 gabions and 107 fascines.[362]

Gaskins' Battalion was finally sent into the trenches on October 11. General Steuben stressed that the men must remain on alert and pay attention to their duty. Corporal Philip King of Captain Lovely's Company recalled that they were engaged in skirmishing almost every day while on the front lines.[363] Private Edward Barker was wounded in the foot during the siege and was unable to continue in the service.[364] Private John Davis of Captain Nathan Lamme's Company experienced a close brush with death while on the front lines:

> *One night, whilst on guard had my gun Barril in my hands About half cut off By the Bursting of a Bum* [bomb] *shell. It set my clothes on fire. I was much stunned and shocked, and remained speechless and senseless for*

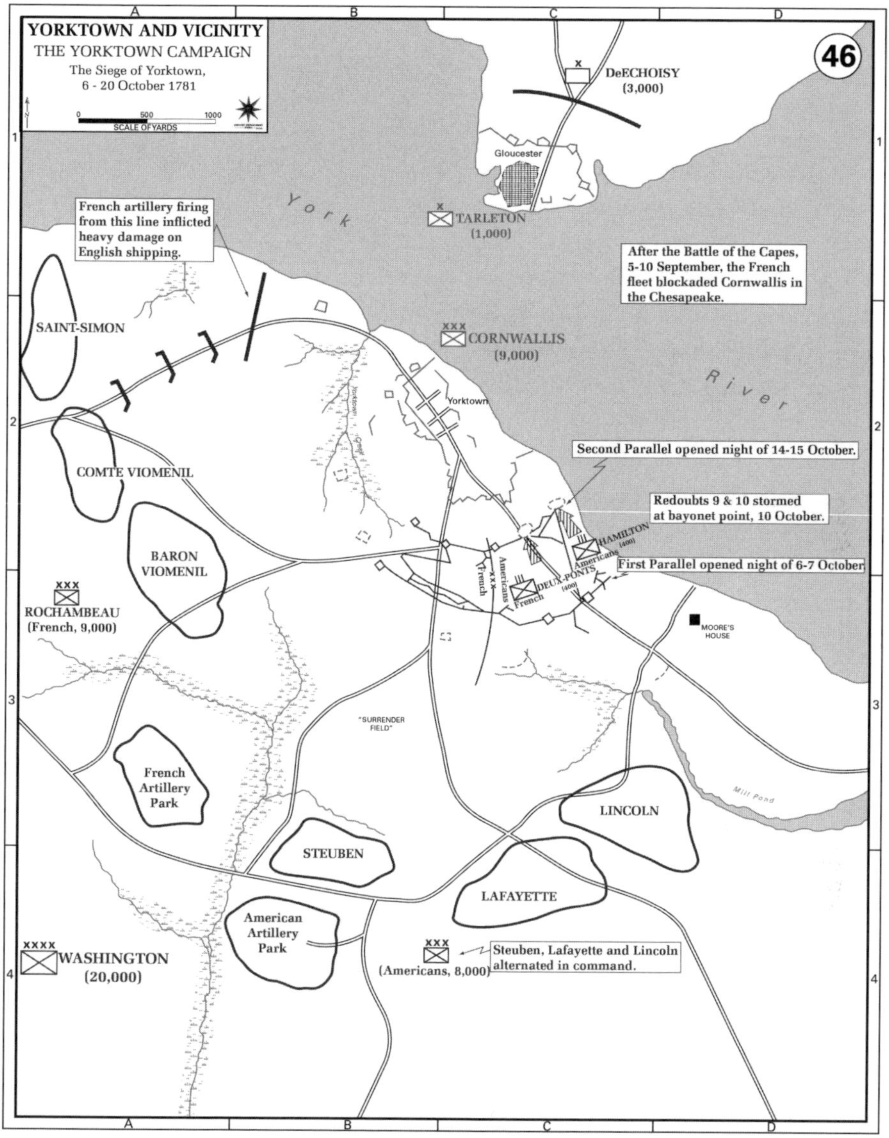


*Opposite, top*: Nelson House, Yorktown, Virginia. *Detroit Publishing Co.; William Henry Jackson, photographer; between 1900 and 1906. Library of Congress.*

*Opposite, bottom*: The Thomas Nelson house (*right*), in Yorktown, Virginia; it was used as a hospital and, in 1781, as a headquarters by Lord Cornwallis. *Between 1860 and 1865. Library of Congress.*

*Above*: Map of the Siege of Yorktown. *Courtesy of the United States Military Academy Department of History.*

> *some time, untill the balance of the Guard came to my relief & put out the fire Burning my cloths. I then recovered not experiencing much injury from the* [shock].[365]

Another veteran, Private John Bradshaw of Captain Lovely's Company, recalled that his brother Robert went into the enemy's lines and brought two horses across the lines to give to officers in the battalion.[366] On the night of October 14, Gaskins' Battalion was stationed in reserve to be prepared to support the assaults on redoubts no. 9 and no. 10. Some of the Virginians were attached to the assault column led by Colonel Alexander Hamilton. Corporal Philip King described how he and others were ordered that "the flints were taken out of our guns and we took the redout at the point of the Bayonet."[367] After an attempt to escape across the York River was disrupted by a storm, Cornwallis had no choice but to surrender. Gaskins' Battalion was in the trenches when the surrender took place, so as part of the protocol of eighteenth-century siege warfare, they remained in their positions as the British army marched from their fortifications to lay down their arms. The men of the battalion were proud of their service in the siege as the last major engagement of the American Revolution. Private William Candler of

The taking of Yorktown. *Vve. Turgis, circa 1840. Library of Congress.*

Captain John Overton's Company commented on the siege in his pension application of 1832:

> *His time having expired before the surrender of Cornwallis; although he did not leave the Army until after that surrender, which he was at, and worked harder in the trenches at Yorktown than he ever did any where else, during the same length of time, in his life.*[368]

Despite the victory at Yorktown, two years remained in the war. With Virginia cleared of British troops, the focus again turned toward General Greene and securing the South. Greene still needed more troops to gain control of the remainder of South Carolina and Georgia, and the enlistments of most of the Virginia Brigade would expire at the end of the year. Lieutenant Colonel Gaskins returned to his home in Northumberland County to stay on a permanent furlough. The men of Gaskins' Battalion were destined to receive a new commander and had still more trials to suffer through before peace was had.

Chapter 7

# THE LAST CAMPAIGNS

## Formation of Posey's Battalion

Thomas Posey had recently been promoted to lieutenant colonel, in September 1781. Between occasionally commanding militia at different times throughout 1780 and 1781, Posey had been placed in charge of gathering recruits in the Shenandoah Valley region. In August, he was ordered to report to a new rendezvous station, Cumberland Old Courthouse. Located in Powhatan County, the "courthouse" was the tavern of Littleberry Mosby. Continental troops had encamped there and at nearby Powhatan Courthouse briefly in May before they were forwarded to Point of Fork. It had also served as a rendezvous point for Continental dragoons in July.[369] Colonel Febiger was placed as commander of the station but left to bring his wife from Philadelphia, so Posey was in temporary command for the months of September and October.[370] Despite this, Posey also left the station to witness the surrender at Yorktown, making him one of the few Americans to witness the two large surrenders of British troops during the American Revolution, Saratoga and Yorktown.

General Washington had planned on sending Gaskins' Battalion to join General Greene immediately after the siege at Yorktown, but Colonel Febiger and General Steuben convinced him to keep them in Virginia to be reorganized. Febiger reported, "The whole of those present I find on Examination to be almost totally destitute of Cloathing and entirely unfit to proceed on a long March."[371] Febiger proposed that Gaskins' Battalion,

Surrender of Cornwallis at Yorktown. *François Godefroy, artist, and Nicolas Ponce, 1784. Library of Congress.*

Surrender of Cornwallis, 1914. *Library of Congress.*

led by Major Poulson, march to Cumberland Old Courthouse to join Lieutenant Colonel Posey, who had gathered 170 soldiers there. Once there, Febiger would select the men with the longest terms to serve to be placed under Posey and marched south. The men with shorter terms would serve the remainder of their enlistment in Virginia with Febiger.[372] Washington approved the plan, and Poulson led the Virginians out of Yorktown on October 24. Captain Nathan Lamme was left with a company of men whose enlistments expired in December to guard prisoners there before they were moved further inland.[373] Some of the men followed the prisoners to Winchester Barracks and remained as guards there.[374]

Gaskins' Battalion marched into camp at Cumberland Old Courthouse on November 2, lacking many officers. Febiger complained that four of the eight companies lacked any officers to command them.[375] Morale was extremely low. Lieutenant William Eskridge, the adjutant of the battalion, called it "the most ruinous of any regiment in the Army of the United States."[376] Besides lack of clothing, the new battalion was suffering from illness, desertions and Major Poulson's liberal furloughs, from which "very few of them have ever returned."[377] Colonel Febiger despised Major Poulson. Although Poulson was a veteran of five years and had spent time as a prisoner of war following the Battle of Germantown, Febiger saw him as an inefficient officer. He referred to Poulson as a "cursed fool" and criticized everything about him, including his grammar and spelling.[378] Febiger complained that because of Poulson's liberal furloughs of both enlisted men and officers, only two hundred men with six officers reported to Cumberland Old Courthouse.

The disorder that reigned in the Virginia Continentals stationed in Virginia was sorted out on November 9. As he had tried to do with Gaskins' Battalion, Febiger ordered the men into companies based on regiments. Eight companies were reorganized, numbered one through eight to represent each regiment of the Virginia Continental Line that existed on paper.[379] Captain Parker's company of Charleston veterans was also attached to the new battalion. Their stay was short, however, as they were granted furloughs through December, as promised in the summer. Parker's company, all veteran soldiers, was assigned as the light infantry company of the battalion. Lieutenant Colonel Posey took command of the battalion, while Major Samuel Finley was assigned as his second-in-command. Febiger did not like the officers of Posey's Battalion. He had written to Colonel William Davies about the men of Gaskins' Battalion that he "pitied the men, and damn'd the O—, a very few only excepted."[380] The officers added to Colonel Febiger's headache, though, with a petition soon after arriving at Cumberland.

On November 16, 1781, the officers presented a memorandum of their condition to Colonel Febiger, with the intention for it to be forwarded to the Virginia General Assembly. In the first part of the memorandum, the men complained of pain, as some of the officers had not been paid for two or three years.[381] "We are truly destitute of cloathing," the officers wrote in the memorandum, "having barely sufficient to support us against the inclemencies of a Winter Campaign, nor has each officer a Blankett."[382] The officers felt insulted by the lack of pay and clothing but wished to serve their country. They had no objection to being sent to South Carolina, but they wanted to be sent properly clothed and paid. Toward the end of the memorandum, they claimed they had been treated differently than their brothers in arms from other states:

> *Lett them cast their Eyes on our Sister States to the northward of us and see how amply, they have provided for those brave Officers and Men, who have fought their Battles and indured with perseverance the innumerable hardships attending on the military profession—Then lett them draw a Line, by which they will see, that the Ballance of ill Usage and Neglect has fallen with unmerciful Weight on the shoulders of the Officers of the Virga continental Line in a many fold proportion to that of the Sufferings of Officers in any other State in the Union.*[383]

Until the conditions of the officers and men were improved, the officers threatened to resign rather than march to South Carolina. The memorandum was signed by the five most senior officers at Cumberland Old Courthouse on the behalf of the officers, including Posey and Finley.[384] The memorandum was sent to the General Assembly and to General Arthur St. Clair (who commanded the Pennsylvanians who were sent to South Carolina), who then forwarded it to General Washington. Washington was both surprised and disappointed by the Virginia officers' memorandum. He placed fault on the undisciplined nature of the enlisted men on the officers and asked in a letter to Febiger, "What can they expect from their soldiers, when they themselves strike at the root of authority and discipline?"[385] Washington wrote that he was embarrassed by the refusal of the Virginians to march south and made it clear that they were destined to march whether they agreed or not, though he hoped to see the state clothe and pay them.

## Final Campaign of the Virginia Brigade

While Febiger tried to clothe and organize Posey's Battalion, the Virginia Brigade continued to serve in the South. Major Snead remained in command of the brigade, with Captain Edmonds commanding the First Virginia and Major Snead remaining as the nominal commander of the Second Virginia. The officer corps continued to suffer, as many officers fell to illness or, due to wounds, desired to go home. Ensign Daniel Ball, who was disabled by a musket ball in his left leg, requested on September 26, 1781, to be allowed to retire because he had lost the use of that leg.[386] He asked General Greene to help him secure a couple of horses for him to ride home along with another sick officer, Lieutenant Peterfield Archer. The brigade itself did not have more than three hundred officers and men present and fit for service after the battle at Eutaw Springs. Though it was referred to as a brigade, it appears that after Eutaw Springs, the First and Second Virginia operated in the field as one battalion.[387]

The Southern Army remained encamped on the High Hills of the Santee through the month of November. The Virginians returned to their steady life of drill and guard duty, while General Greene and South Carolina Governor John Rutledge tried to pacify the Loyalists and set up a new elected state government. With the British evacuation of Wilmington, North Carolina, on November 14, Greene hoped to compel the remaining British forces in South Carolina into Charleston. Governor Rutledge also hoped for Greene to advance again against the British, freeing up more territory for the legislative election in the state. The South Carolina militia under General Sumter were focused on capturing Loyalists under Major William "Bloody Bill" Cunningham and left Greene with most of his Continentals to march against Charleston. Greene marched his forces out of the High Hills on November 19, with the intention to drive any British forces into the city of Charleston.

The men of the Virginia Brigade marched out with Greene's army wearing new brown regimental coats with brown facings.[388] Some of the men received more comfortable clothing—woolen overalls—on November 30 while encamped at Orangeburg.[389] Some of the Virginians were then attached to the light infantry of Lee's Legion and were led by Greene, accompanied by Continental cavalry, in the direction of Dorchester.[390] They formed a separate company led by Captain Sigismund Stribling.[391] The march on Dorchester was one of the worst the Virginians were involved in, as General Greene later reported in a letter to President Thomas McKean of the Continental Congress:

> *We arrived here on the 1st of this Instant, after one of the most disagreeable marches I ever made; the swamps being full, the rivers high and the face of the Country almost all covered with water. It was my intention to have surprised the place, but passing through a very disaffected part of the Country the enemy got intelligence of our approach the night before our arrival.*[392]

The British burned most of their supplies at Dorchester before they withdrew to the Charleston Neck by the next day. The Virginia light infantrymen with Lee's Legion watched the area between the Ashley and Edisto Rivers, while South Carolina troops led by General Marion watched the area between the Ashley and Cooper Rivers.[393] General Greene marched the remainder of his army to Round O, South Carolina, which was roughly thirty miles from where the British were building new earthworks along Goose Creek. Although this advance did not result in heavy fighting, it signaled the end of British control in South Carolina. For the remainder of the conflict, British territorial control was limited to the city of Charleston and the immediate area, and they had to rely on raids into American-held territory. This, however, did not eliminate the Loyalist raiders in the backcountry or the Native warriors of the Cherokee and Creek tribes from attacking American forces and settlements. Greene would spend the remainder of the conflict trying to defeat these forces and retain control.

Besides service in Lee's Legion, more Virginians were detached to serve in a new light infantry force. Colonel John Laurens of South Carolina was placed in charge of gathering information for the Southern Army and took command of the light infantry of the Southern Army, including those belonging to Lee's Legion. A detachment of Delaware and Virginia Continentals was placed under Laurens' command on December 19.[394] They were first stationed at Parker's Ferry to watch the British forces at Charleston. These Virginians remained under the command of Lieutenant Ballard Smith.[395] The remainder of the brigade settled into their winter quarters at Round O. The men of the Virginia Brigade were ordered to be drilled twice a day by battalions. General Greene also permitted the men to take out limited ammunition to go hunting to provide meat rations. Not all who left the camp, however, left with good intentions. On December 10, three soldiers of the Virginia Brigade and two men of the Maryland Brigade were found guilty of being absent without leave and plundering the inhabitants of the region and sentenced to "run the Gauntlet line through the whole Army" later that evening.[396] The Virginians also performed duty at Stono Ferry, where they watched the British forces there.[397]

John Laurens. *National Portrait Gallery, Washington, D.C.; Smithsonian Institution.*

The encampment of the Virginia Brigade was short-lived. As most of the men had been enlisted in the summer of 1780 for eighteen months service, their enlistment was over on December 31. The only Virginians who remained in the Southern Army were those who were attached to Lieutenant Smith's light infantry company. Major Snead and the remainder of the brigade were replaced by North Carolina Continentals at Stono Ferry. The men gave up their accoutrements and arms to the conductor of military arms to supply deficiencies in the Maryland and North Carolina regiments. General Greene thanked the officers and men of the Virginia Brigade "for their long faithful and hard services which they have performed to so much advantage to their Country and honor to themselves."[398] Marching over the same ground they had marched and fought over for the past year, the men marched to Salisbury, North Carolina. On January 18, 1782, Major Snead ordered that the men be discharged from there, and the Virginia Brigade, which had covered over one thousand miles over the course of the campaign, ceased to exist.[399]

## THE WINTER ENCAMPMENT OF CUMBERLAND OLD COURTHOUSE

With the dissolution of the Virginia Brigade, General Greene needed troops to replace them. The Pennsylvania Line arrived four days after the Virginians left, but this was still a smaller force than what was needed to control South Carolina and Georgia, let alone retake the major cities of Savannah and Charleston. Greene wrote continuously to Governor Benjamin Harrison and Colonel Christian Febiger about the need for Lieutenant Colonel Posey's Battalion in the South. Posey's men had gone through their own trials over the winter of 1782.

Shortly after the arrival of the soldiers who had served at Yorktown, evidence of a smallpox outbreak became apparent. In an attempt to prevent the spread of smallpox in the camp, Colonel Febiger proposed inoculations take place at Cumberland Old Courthouse. The locals of Powhatan County received information about this plan and fervently opposed it. These locals were concerned about the spread of smallpox to the community if any soldier carried the disease into the countryside. A petition signed by thirty-two landowners from the county was prepared and given to Febiger by Littleberry Mosby Sr., who was the owner of the tavern at the encampment and a county official. During the conversation, Colonel Febiger recalled, Mosby "spoke of loaded guns" and used "some very imprudent expressions."[400] The inoculations didn't take place at Cumberland Old Courthouse.

The men were steadily uniformed (though not adequately) and disciplined according to Steuben's tactics. While they were disciplined in drill, they were not the same in the camps. Richard Neale was found guilty on November 6 of "drunkenness and attempting to force a centinal when on duty" and was sentenced to receive one hundred lashes.[401] William Campen and John Henley were tried on November 30, 1781, for breaking into a mill owned by General Charles Scott and sentenced to receive one hundred lashes each.[402] John Crouch, who was proven to be a British deserter, was ordered to be "beat out with the Rouges March [down] the main road leading down the country" on December 17, 1781.[403] On the night of November 16, 1781, "no less than three large fat hogs and nine turkeys" were stolen; Colonel Febiger ordered that the roll be called four times every day, and any man found absent would be punished with fifty lashes without a court martial.[404] A similar order was given when it was discovered that the men were burning fence rails for fuel. To keep men in the camp and prevent desertion, Febiger sent numerous patrols into the countryside and increased guards around the camp. Only one death sentence was carried out in the camp: Joseph Hawkins, a "mulatto" who had enlisted for the duration of the war in June 1781, was found guilty of plundering several homes and was hanged before the entire camp on February 9, 1782.[405]

Supplies were also an issue within the camp. Although blue regimental coats arrived in December, they came without buttons; this was solved by melting down musket balls to be molded into buttons.[406] Food supplies came to a crisis point in the first month of 1782. The last substantial meat ration came on Christmas Day, when each men received half a pound of meat for a Christmas meal. Soon after New Year's, however, there was no meat in the camp. The soldiers went through twelve days without meat ration before beef was brought from Amelia County, though it was in no condition to be issued. The meat had been fresh but was not preserved in salt, so it had turned foul. Febiger attempted to issue the meat to the men, and some of the men complained so loudly that Febiger had them confined. On January 20,

150 soldiers rose up in arms and began to march to the blockhouse to free the men. Only the "vigilance of the officers," as Colonel Febiger reported to Colonel Davies three days later, prevented the men from storming the blockhouse.[407] Beef was also brought in shortly afterward from Richmond, but Febiger feared more protests would follow if he issued this beef; he stated that it was "dangerous to be near."[408]

On January 26, 1782, Febiger informed the officers and men of Posey's Battalion that they were to march south as soon as proper supplies were issued, adding in his orders that he thought the men would go "cheerfully" to the aid of General Greene. The enlisted men of Posey's Battalion were the opposite of cheerful. A piece of paper was found in the camp that encouraged a mutiny to prevent the march. Inspections of the men on February 4 and 10 found that the men were "not yet well clad," but still planned to march the men to South Carolina.[409] Wagons were prepared for the march, and Febiger hoped that Posey's Battalion would help to "retrieve the sinking caracter of the Va Line."[410]

On the morning of February 14, Posey's Battalion and a company of Continental artillery were formed on the parade ground, where Lieutenant Colonel Posey read the orders for the battalion to march out. The men were dismissed to collect their gear. The "General" was beaten by the drummers later that morning, and officers fully expected the men to collect their knapsacks and form for the march. To their surprise, the men appeared on the parade ground with their muskets but no other equipment. After months of being poorly clothed, sickly, underfed and underpaid, the enlisted men had decided that this was the last straw; the solution was mutiny. Even as officers and some of the sergeants shouted at the men to gather their knapsacks, the enlisted men remained in formation.[411] Colonel Febiger reported to Washington that it took "a letter threatening some persuasion and an excellent band of music to play them off" before the soldiers marched out. Febiger described the same event to Colonel Davies but in a different manner:

> *On the 14th inst: I got rid of the said Detachment after hanging one and whipping 73 of them, and they are well officer'd and Posey informs me behave well on their march. I dismounted the Officers, which has a good Effect.*[412]

Lieutenant Francis Brooke, who commanded the Continental artillery that was also sent south, reported that one of the officers, Captain Clough

Posey's Virginia Battalion, circa 1782. *Courtesy of Don Troiani.*

Shelton, ran a sword through a sergeant's body during the mutiny and that Colonel Febiger ordered the barracks to be set on fire.[413] Regardless of the account, the result was the same: Lieutenant Colonel Posey and his battalion of 441 officers and men left from Cumberland Old Courthouse to serve in the Southern Army.[414]

## Service in Georgia and the Capture of Charleston

The mood of Posey's Battalion changed once they marched south. Lieutenant Colonel Posey reported that "the Spirit, which seem'd to possess them just before our March is in a great manner subsided" and that "Chearfullness appears in the men's Countenances."[415] Their spirits were also lifted by the arrival of rum while they encamped near Prince Edward Courthouse on February 17. Posey reported on how the men received this welcome ration:

> *Last Evening the Rum came up, I issued a Gill to every man; But not having had any so long some of them gott very Tipsey on their Gill, though none acted out of Caracter except one or two, the Deserters amount only to three; I have not a Doubt of marching every man now with the Detachement to general Greene's Army.*[416]

Two weeks later, Colonel Posey's men stopped at Salisbury, North Carolina, bogged down by spring rains and the need to impress food from the citizens.[417] Many of the men were now barefoot as well, so Posey marched the battalion to Charlotte in hopes of receiving food and shoes there. On their arrival on March 16, Posey found that neither food nor shoes were stockpiled at Charlotte. After marching from Charlotte, General Greene ordered Lieutenant Colonel Posey not to join the Southern Army at Round O but to proceed to Georgia to join the command of General Wanye, consisting of 270 Continental dragoons from the First Continental Light Dragoons, as well as Georgia militia cavalry and infantry. The mission of Wayne's force was to prevent further raids from Savannah, Georgia. On April 7, Posey's Battalion joined General Wanye at Ebenezer, Georgia, located roughly twenty-five miles from Savannah. General Wayne was pleased by the arrival of the Virginians, declaring that the men "are equal to my most sanguine wishes, as I believe both Officers and men are second to none in the American Army!"[418]

The next month, Posey's men proved their discipline and fighting prowess in skirmishes outside Savannah. On May 21, the men of Captain Parker's light infantry company were engaged in a skirmish against Loyalists at Harris' Bridge. Lieutenant Colonel Thomas Brown led a detachment of 350 infantry and a squadron of cavalry to meet with Creek Indians outside of Savannah and escort them into the city. They were unable to make contact, and Brown turned back to the city. General Wayne, with 500 men and three three-pounders, moved to stop him. Parker's Company was sent in advance with a section of dragoons to seize a causeway and prevent the retreat of Brown's men. Parker was ordered to cut through woods and swamps to reach the causeway, and once his men had engaged Brown's, they were to hold their fire and "to fall upon [them] with sword and bayonet."[419] After capturing most of a Loyalist patrol, the dragoons and Parker's men attacked the vanguard of Brown's force. Brown and his men were formed in a column on the causeway, and the Virginians' attack put the column into retreat toward Savannah. The attack and rout took place so quickly that Wayne was unable to move his force into place to prevent a retreat and capture the entire force, though Wayne noted, "The few of our Troops that had an Opportunity to engage introduced the American Sword and bayonet with such effects as to kill many and wound some."[420] Parker's men captured one officer and eighteen dragoons in the skirmish and killed and wounded several others, while losing two men killed and three wounded.[421] Night and the fact that the enemy had fled into the swamps made pursuit impossible. The Virginians were paraded in sight of Savannah the next day to draw the British into battle, skirmishing at night with the garrison.[422]

A month later, General Wayne's men encamped about five miles from Savannah. At the same time, a force of three hundred Creek warriors led by Chief Emistisiguo tried to move past Wayne's force but ultimately decided to attack the picket guard at Sharon, another plantation owned by William Gibbons. Unknown to Emistisiguo, Wayne had moved his camp to Sharon Plantation on June 22. Captain Parker's light infantry company, after having been in front of Savannah for several days, was sent to the rear of the camp to rest near the artillery. Around three o'clock in the morning on June 23, the Creek warriors launched their attack, killing a sentinel after he fired a shot to warn the camp. Captain Parker's company was roused from their sleep and retreated toward Wayne's headquarters at the plantation house, where they joined the quarter guard. Lieutenant Colonel Posey helped rally the guards and Parker's men, while Major Finley was ordered to bring up the battalion from behind the house. Wayne and Parker led the rallied men in a bayonet

"Colonial soldiers engaged in battle in a forest, possibly during the American Revolution." *Detroit Publishing Co., publisher; Milwaukee Public Museum. Library of Congress.*

charge against the Creek warriors "through a most tremendous fire of small Arms accompanied by a hedious Yell from almost every direction."[423] Posey and Finley led the battalion on the flank of the Creek warriors and forced the warriors to retreat. The infantrymen were joined by the attack of the First Continental Dragoons, led by Major James Gunn.

Posey recalled that "the charge was made with celerity and firmness, though the conflict was severe, many of the Indians [fell] by the force of the bayonet."[424] Private Reuben Brizendine witnessed General Wayne's horse being killed; Wayne continued on foot in the fighting.[425] Posey himself felled one or more warriors with his own swords. Unfortunately, in the confusion of the fighting, Posey also struck down Corporal Flanders Thompson of Captain Parker's company, who had taken off his coat and tied up his head with a handkerchief, contrary to orders.[426] Thompson survived his wounds and was furloughed home to Virginia for the remainder of the war. Corporal William Rhodes of Parker's Company was severely wounded by shots through his left shoulder and left hand, though he continued to serve until the next summer.[427]

After Emistisiguo was killed trying to turn the artillery against the Americans, the remaining warriors fled, and the skirmish was an American victory. Eighteen warriors were found killed alongside Emistisiguo, while the Americans reported twelve killed and wounded total. Private Joseph

Walton of Captain Shelton's Company claimed that twenty-six warriors were killed.[428] Twelve warriors were captured by Lieutenant Colonel Posey, who brought the men into camp. General Wanye learned of the prisoners and ordered them put to death. Posey protested the order but unsuccessfully, so the prisoners were put to death.[429] On July 11, Savannah was evacuated and occupied by General Wayne's forces. Captain Parker's light infantry was marched from the city to meet Loyalist forces led by Lieutenant Colonel Thomas "Burn Foot" Brown at Skidaway Island in late July, but Brown had withdrawn after engaging Georgia militia on July 25. On August 12, Posey's Battalion marched with General Wayne to join the Southern Army in South Carolina. They remained stationed at Ashley Hill Plantation, where they performed picket duty near James Island. Private Lott Bearcroft of Captain Thomas Martin's Company deserted from picket duty and went to the British camp on the island.[430]

## Peace at Last

While Posey's Battalion was campaigning in Georgia, the Virginia Continentals, led by Lieutenant Ballard Smith, were engaged in scouting and skirmishes around Charleston. Lieutenant Smith made a name for himself in the operations with Lee's Legion, including one mission where he led twelve men to take officers at Dewee's Tavern, located two miles from Charleston. It was a popular place for British officers, and Smith was determined to see who he could capture there. After one of the sergeants detached from Lee's Legion scouted out the property, he returned to Smith, who waited with the men in a boat with muffled oars. The next night, Smith and his men returned to capture the officers. In 1822, Alexander Garden, a veteran of Lee's Legion, recounted what happened next:

> *The following night being favorable to enterprise, the reiver was passed as before, and the boat, steered by* [Sergeant] *DuCoin, made the landing, Lieutenant Smith immediately surrounding the house, entered it, in full expectation of making a handsome capture of officers, but his evil genius forbade it. Instead of twenty or thirty officers, many of them of high rank, a Hessian Major, and a Lieutenant of the volunteers of Ireland, who had sacrificed too freely to Bacchus, were the only persons found on premises. These he parolled, and returned without molestation.*[431]

Around the same time, Ensign John Foster of the same company was stationed at the Fuller Plantation near Ashley Ferry. Foster found a British armed vessel opposite the plantation with intentions of raiding the area. He hid his eighteen men in the marsh and waited for the raiders to land. Alexander Garden offered an account of events:

> *The marauders advancing in their boat, never suspected their danger till they saw the muskets of eighteen men, within ten yards, directly levelled at them. One man snatched up a blunderbuss and would have resisted, had he not been restrained by his companions, who, calling loudly for quarter, surrendered at discretion. This was a very acceptable prize. A fine boat, completely equipped, well provided with comforts, and twenty six prisoners, well-armed, surrendered without a shot being fired.... Their captivity was of short duration. Colonel Laurens, who commanded in the neighbourhood, sent them in their own boat, under a sanction of a flag of truce, to Charleston, making them the heralds of their own disgrace.*[432]

Following the evacuation of Savannah, the city of Charleston became the last British stronghold in the South. While peace was negotiated, General Alexander Leslie, the British commander at Charleston, was ordered to begin the process of evacuating the city. Leslie lacked enough ships to begin the evacuation, so it was delayed until December. In the meantime, Leslie still had to rely on raids into the countryside to supply his force. He sent an offer to buy supplies from General Greene's Army, which Greene denied. Leslie sent a force to find supplies along the Combahee River. In response, Greene sent his light infantry force, led by General Mordecai Gist, to oppose the raiding parties. Lieutenant Smith's Company of Virginia Continentals was still in service under Colonel Laurens and went along on the expedition. On August 27, Laurens' force was ambushed by British troops about one mile from Chehaw Point, and Laurens himself was mortally wounded. Some of the Virginians were present in the engagement, as well as some from the recently arrived Posey's Battalion, although none were among the two killed and nineteen wounded.[433]

General Greene moved his army to Ashley Hill Plantation to be closer to Charleston. In October, the British exchanged the remaining prisoners kept at Charleston, including many Virginians who had been captured during the siege there and the 1781 campaign.[434] Most of these men had served a long time. Private John Palmer was captured in a skirmish after Eutaw Springs and spent eleven months aboard the British prison ship *Eske* before

Major General Nathanael Greene. *Miriam and Ira D. Wallach Division of Art, Prints and Photographs: Print Collection, New York Public Library Digital Collections.*

he was exchanged on October 24. He had been drafted for eighteen months' service from Loudoun County in October 1780, so he was discharged by General Greene when he arrived at Ashley Hill. These Virginia Continentals were not the only ones to depart from the South at that time. Many of the enlistments of the men in Posey's Battalion expired in September and October 1782. Lieutenant Colonel Posey led 185 officers and men from the camp on October 1, their destination being Cumberland Old Courthouse. These troops arrived there in November and were discharged from service.[435] Major Finley was left in command of those who remained. The battalion was reorganized into three companies, led by Captains Alexander Parker, Henry Moss and Clough Shelton. The men who made up Finley's reorganized battalion were all enlisted for either three years or the duration of the war and were all veteran soldiers. Not all who remained, though, wanted to remain much longer. Private Larkin Doggin of Captain Moss' Company deserted from the camp on December 8. Battalion muster rolls dated December 11, 1782, indicate that of the 226 officers and men in service, 143 were present and fit for service. These men of Finley's Battalion were part of the American force that marched into Charleston following the British evacuation on December 14, 1782. Captain Parker's Company, consisting of many men who had been captured there in 1780, were among the first into the city that had been the site of their greatest defeat.

Chapter 8

# BECOMING CITIZENS OF A NEW REPUBLIC

## Finley's Men's Final Months in Service

Following the evacuation of Charleston, Major Finley's Battalion marched to James Island, where they constructed winter quarters. Three more men deserted while in camp there in February 1783.[436] Some of the officers also went home. Captain Henry Moss, after having served since the beginning of the war, was "deranged" and allowed to retire from service on February 5, leaving command of the company to Lieutenant Joseph Conway.[437] In April 1783, Finley's Battalion marched back to Savannah to be garrisoned there, accompanied by a company of Continental artillery. Finley's men encamped about four miles below the town, while the artillery was stationed at Fort Wayne.[438] The men were, however, still poorly fed. Though the official peace treaty had not yet been ratified, the preliminary peace treaty was known to everyone, but the State of Georgia seemed unwilling to supply the Virginians with food.

Major Finley attempted to get an impressment warrant from Georgia's Governor Lyman Hall, but Hall refused to grant it. Finley still impressed from the state without a written warrant and decided to wait to be sued by the state government. He also wrote that he would march his men anywhere else in Georgia at the governor's request but that "unless a Contractor or an Agent was to attend us, for the people of that and its neighbouring Countries have Associated together to oppose, by force of arms, any parties that may dare to impress provisions from them."[439] He added that he believed "a combination of the whole state" was against the Continentals. "The General cry is they are ruined," Finley wrote, "yet their harbour is constantly crouded with flagg vessels from St. Augustine who return loaded with every species of provisions for that Garrison."[440] Some of the enlisted men possibly felt that they'd be better off going home, for six men from Captain Shelton's Company deserted in the month of May, including a sergeant and a musician.[441]

The last assignment the Virginians received came when General Wayne negotiated a treaty with the Cherokee and Creek tribes at Augusta, Georgia, in April 1783. General Wayne ordered Finley's Battalion to appear and act as guards during the negotiations. Lieutenant Brooke went along and remarked on a peculiar order from General Wayne:

> *While in Savannah the troops were ordered to an Indian treaty at Augusta, and we were ordered to turn out with whiskers and moustaches; this I was too young to do, being then not nineteen years old; but I used some black pomatum, such as the Hessian jägers used, and smeared my face, so as to look very ferocious. The Indians were frightened by their defeat by General Wayne.*[442]

After the attack on Wayne's camp at Gibbon's Plantation and the subsequent execution of twelve prisoners by men of Captain Joseph Scott's Company of Posey's Battalion, the Cherokee and Creek Natives were frightened by the Virginians and told Wayne that they would attend no negotiations if the Virginians were at Augusta.[443] Although most of Finley's men were sent away, Captain Parker, Lieutenant Nathaniel Darby and forty-six men remained with Wayne during the treaty negotiations.[444] The remainder of the men had gathered back in Charleston, South Carolina, by the end of June 1783.

In June 1783, General Greene received orders from Secretary of War Benjamin Lincoln to furlough the remaining Virginians under his command. The Continental Army was in the process of disbanding, and the men were being furloughed to save on provisions; they were to be discharged later once word of the official peace treaty arrived. Although they were offered transport, these transports were not prepared, and many men of the battalion were allowed to march back to Virginia once given enough food from General Greene. These men were marched to Richmond, Virginia, where they were discharged in late June.[445] On July 12, 1783, some of the men of Finley's Battalion, in addition to other Continental troops amounting to over four hundred officers and men, embarked on transports and sailed along the coast to Virginia. The remaining men of the battalion reported to Richmond after making a stop for a celebration at Hampton in August and were discharged, ending the story of the battalion led by Posey and Finley.[446]

## The Last of the Virginia Continental Line

Although major fighting had ended in Virginia following the victory at Yorktown, Virginia Continentals remained to perform duties across the state. On the Eastern Shore, Captain Thomas Parker commanded a company of Continentals recruited from Accomack and Northampton Counties. These soldiers remained on the Eastern Shore for most of 1781 to perform guard duty against British and Loyalist raiders. This company was brought to Cumberland Old Courthouse during the spring of 1782.[447] Colonel Febiger remained as commander of the Cumberland Old Courthouse station, which was designated as the general rendezvous for Virginia recruits. Other stations, such as Albemarle Old Courthouse and Fredericksburg, remained as regional rendezvous stations for the men before they were forwarded to Cumberland Old Courthouse. With the preliminary peace treaty in the fall of 1782, the remaining Continentals in Virginia were ordered to remain in the state and marched to Winchester to guard the Yorktown prisoners.[448] The troops remained encamped there until July 1783.

The prisoners from Yorktown were removed to be escorted to New York, where they were released to the British army, and the Continentals were no longer needed at Winchester. After discharging nearly all the three-year enlisted men, General Muhlenberg ordered the remaining Continentals to Point of Fork to act as guards at the arsenal there.[449] On September 10, 1783, Captain William Johnson, the commandant of the Virginia troops at Point of Fork, furloughed all the men to go home until called into service again.[450] Peace was declared a few months later, and the men were considered discharged from service. After eight years of war, the Virginia Continental Line was finally disbanded and passed into history.

## Life as Veterans

Once the men were discharged from service or furloughed, those who served until the end had to find their way home. Private Oliver Wallace, a veteran of Guilford Courthouse and Yorktown, was discharged from Williamsburg in November 1781. He was given no final pay and "begged his way home barefooted" with "his clothes nearly worn off" as he made his way to Rockingham County.[451] Samuel Allen had to beg his way home as well, walking from Salisbury, North Carolina, to Augusta County.[452] Andrew Keyser, a veteran of Greene's Southern Army, was discharged at Salisbury with the remainder of the brigade. In lieu of pay, Captain Edmonds gave a pay certificate to Keyser, and he made his way to Rockbridge County.[453] Veteran Tapley Lightfoot later recalled the condition he was in on his return home:

> *At the time of his discharge applicant had neither hat, coat, shoes nor stockings, his whole apparel consisting of a pair of flaxen trousers and a shirt of his own making. In this condition it is not surprising that he lost these papers. They never reached home with him.*[454]

Private James Cox of Posey's Battalion recalled a similar experience in 1782:

> *At that time our officers concluded that as our soldiers were in so destitute a situation that they had not the means of getting home, they would not disband them until they were marched to Virginia, they were accordingly marched by two Captains to Carters Ferry in Va. where he with all the others was discharged.*[455]

Others had some misfortune during their return home. Private Lewis Griffin, who fought with Lieutenant Campbell's Battalion at Guilford Courthouse, remained at the courthouse to aid his wounded brother. In October 1781, he and his brother were permitted by a surgeon to return home and were given written furloughs.[456] He was given permission to remain home until notified to return to the army. The Battle of Yorktown was fought before they reached home, and he was never called back into service. Griffin could not produce the furloughs during his pension declaration in 1832, because he had placed them in his pocketbook, which was stolen with his coat while he was on the way home.[457]

Many of the men faded into the background of society when they returned home. Some saw military service later in their lives. Lieutenant William Evans, who had been wounded three times during his military service, also served as an officer in the Virginia Militia during the Whiskey Rebellion.[458] In the 1790s, Thomas Posey became a brigadier general in the Legion of the

United States, where he served under another Continental veteran, Anthony Wayne. Veteran James Martin also survived the disaster of St. Clair's Defeat in 1791 and subsequently served under General Wayne as well, in the Northwest Indian War.[459] At least one veteran served in the War of 1812: John Short, who fought in the light infantry at Hobkirk's Hill, volunteered in Colonel Johnson's Mounted Kentucky Volunteers Regiment.[460]

Some veterans did take advantage of land bounties to move out of Virginia. A survey of 507 Continental veterans (both officers and enlisted men) showed that 215, or roughly 58 percent, moved out of the state following the American Revolution. Over one-fifth of the men moved to Kentucky; Tennessee and Ohio were the second and third most popular states. The veterans ended up spread over a total of seventeen states and Washington, D.C., with some going as far south as Georgia and as far north as New York and Massachusetts. The enlisted men were more likely to move out of Virginia than the officers. Only one-fifth of the fifty-two officers in the study moved out of Virginia, while well over half of the enlisted men moved to other states. Captain William L. Lovely, an Irishman who served for nearly seven years of the American Revolution, moved to Tennessee after the Revolution and died in 1816 while serving as an Indian agent in Arkansas. Private Robert Owls, a freed man of color who was wounded twice in the South (at Waxhaws and Eutaw Springs), had moved to Opelousas, Louisiana, by the time he applied for his service pension in 1819.[461]

Veterans were not promised pensions unless they were disabled. Disabled veterans such as Private John Stadner, who lost the use of his arm and two fingers, applied for a disability pension from the General Assembly in 1784.[462] Sergeant Robert Clark was with Campbell's Battalion at Guilford Courthouse when a musket ball entered his abdomen and passed through his right hip bone. The wound rendered him "¾th disabled from obtaining his subsistence from manual labor" after the Revolution.[463]

Following the inauguration of a veteran of the Virginia Line, James Monroe, who became president in 1817, the first pension act for Continental veterans was ratified, in 1818. Any veteran of the Continental Army or Navy who had served for nine months was eligible for a pension from the federal government. In 1820, the pension law was updated to include a return of the applicant's property to prove their financial need. Veteran John Huffman, after serving his eighteen months in the Second Virginia with Colonel Hawes, remained in South Carolina, and by 1820, he was living in the Edgefield District. He had owned 170 acres of farmland, where he raised cattle and hogs, but at sixty-three years old, he now found it difficult to work the land. Furthermore, he and his wife had an adult child who died and left them with two children to raise. Huffman had received a pension in 1818 for his Continental service but was stricken from the pension roll for being too wealthy. His wife's health was poor, as was his own, and so he applied again in 1820 and attempted to make his case for the need of the pension. In 1825, he went before the court again to plead his case. Since then, he had sold thirty-two acres of land and been told by neighbors to sell more. Huffman was evidently proud of his service and felt entitled to some form of benefit. In his 1825 pension declaration, he wrote:

> *It is a fond desire of his* [that] *as a free man and in a free Country for which freedom he thought and bled to continue to own land enough not only for a house, poor as it is, the small remnant of time on earth now allotted him, but in which to deposit his bones men did, and where now be the moldering remains of his youngest daughter and grandchild and if he could believe that a construction so hard and in human could be placed on the law as to compel him to sell this spot of earth, which he solemnly declares on oath would, after payment of debts, get but a little way towards his support, refuse him....He would be forced to the conclusion on that it is a most unfortunate circumstance for an old and a worn out soldier of the revolution to be cursed with a little poor Land!*[464]

Huffman's pension was reinstated on December 22, 1825, and he continued to receive eight dollars a month until his death on June 25, 1828. Private William Foxworthy of Gaskins' Battalion faced a similar situation. He had received a pension in Fleming County, Kentucky, in 1832 at the age of eighty. The pension was terminated by 1834, however, due to the lack of sufficient comrade testimony to confirm his service. In response, twenty-three citizens of the county signed a petition to testify to Foxworthy's pension, including a veteran named Charles Arnold, who signed the petition as a "compatriot soldier."[465] The pension of $2.50 per month was reinstated in 1836, and Foxworthy died a year later at the age of eighty-five.

Veteran Bartholomew Cyrus served seven of the eight years of the American Revolution, saw service in the South and was discharged as a guard at the Winchester Barracks, but he struggled to receive more than three payments as a veteran living in Buckingham County, Virginia. He submitted a schedule of his property in 1820: one cow, one hog and two beds, which combined had a worth of twenty-eight dollars. On November 21, 1821, Cyrus wrote to President James Monroe and Secretary of War

John C. Calhoun of his service and condition. His letter provided a glimpse into the lives of many veterans forgotten by the country after the Revolution:

> *I served during this time without ever being confined or one lick* [lash of the whip] *which few can say in truth sir look at your records and you'll find this to be truth Sir I have received three draws from the pension you bestowed us then I sent my Schedule and have got no return from it proved before judge Daniel I am upon sufferance I have had the misfortune a few years since to* [lose] *one of my hands by a gun bursting and am troubled at times with* [rheumatic] *pains and my wife worse off than myself I am going on 64 years of age and my wife is near 70 years of age I was a poor boy had nothing but my shirt and pantaloons when I went in to the army. I think it hard for me to suffer now after doing as much for my country as I have and without your assistance am oblige to go to the poor house and I had almost rather died.*[466]

He finally received his pension and continued to receive it until his death in Appomattox County on July 11, 1855, at the age of ninety-seven. Cyrus was the last known veteran from the Virginia Brigade of 1781 and quite possibly the last remaining veteran of the Virginia Continental Line who served after 1780.

In the over 240 years since the last Continental veterans were discharged from service, their history and experiences have been misunderstood. Research over the past two decades has begun to clear away the vines of time that have covered their stories. Although the veterans passed on, they left the stories of their service behind in the form of pension applications and the letters they wrote in an effort to get recognition for their service. These veterans, whether volunteers or forced by circumstance or law to serve, served as regulars—and without the presence of these regular troops, alongside those of Maryland and Delaware, it is uncertain whether victory in the southern states would have been possible. The Viginia Continentals who fought in the final three years deserve the same credit that other Virginia regiments received for the first five years of the Revolution. As Governor Benjamin Harrison wrote to General Greene at the end of the war, "the sufferings of the heroic troops" Greene had led in the South were "too well known to be forgotten."[467]

# NOTES

## *Introduction*

1. Lewis Griffin, 1832 Pension Declaration.
2. Ibid.
3. John Robert Sellers, "The Virginia Continental Line, 1775–1780" (PhD dissertation, Tulane University, 1968), iii.
4. *A Memorial Volume of the Guilford Battle Ground Company* (Reece and Elam, 1893), 6.
5. Ibid., 39.

## *Chapter 1*

6. E.M. Sanchez-Saavedra, *A Guide to Virginia Military Organizations in the American Revolution, 1774–1787* (Heritage Books, 2007), 55.
7. Michael Cecere, *General Peter Muhlenberg: A Virginia Officer of the Continental Line* (Westholme, 2020), 33.
8. Henry A. Muhlenberg, *The Life of Major General Peter Muhlenberg of the Revolutionary Army* (Carey and Hart, 1849), 75.
9. "To George Washington from Brigadier General Anthony Wayne, 17 July 1779," Founders Online, https://founders.archives.gov.
10. "From Thomas Jefferson to J.P.G. Muhlenberg, 12 April 1780," Founders Online, https://founders.archives.gov.
11. Mary Theresa Leiter, *Biographical Sketches of the Generals of the Continental Army of the Revolution* (University Press, 1889), 143.
12. "George Washington to John Jay, 30 June 1779," Founders Online, https://founders.archives.gov.
13. Library of Congress, *Journals of the Continental Congress, 1774–1780*, vol. 17 (1910), 519.
14. Ibid., 613; "To James Madison from David Jameson, 20 September 1780," Founders Online, https://founders.archives.gov.

15. Francis Bernard Heitman, *Historical Register of Officers of the Continental Army During the War of the Revolution* (Press of Nichols, Killam and Maffitt, 1893), 401.
16. "To Thomas Jefferson from John Page, 11 November 1775," Founders Online, https://founders.archives.gov.
17. Heitman, *Historical Register*, 131.
18. "From George Washington to Brigadier General Charles Scott, 5 May 1779," Founders Online, https://founders.archives.gov.
19. William P. Palmer, *Calendar of Virginia State Papers* (R.F. Walker, 1875), 1:319.
20. "To George Washington from Brigadier General William Woodford, 8 March 1780," Founders Online, https://founders.archives.gov.
21. Heitman, *Historical Register*, 187.
22. Ibid.
23. "From George Washington to Colonel William Davies, 16 December 1779," Founders Online, https://founders.archives.gov.
24. "To George Washington from Brigadier General William Woodford, 8 March 1780," Founders Online, https://founders.archives.gov.
25. "William Davies to Colonel Robert Hanson Harrison, March 20, 1780," in *The Life of Brigadier General William Woodford of the American Revolution*, vol. 2, by Catesby Willis Stewart (Whittet and Shepperson, 1973), 1157.
26. "From George Washington to Colonel William Davies, 20 April 1780," Founders Online, https://founders.archives.gov.
27. Richard Frothingham, *Battle of Bunker Hill* (Little, Brown, 1890), 56.
28. Ibid., 86.
29. John T. Posey, *General Thomas Posey: Son of the American Revolution* (Michigan State University Press, 1992), 58.
30. Holdridge Ozro Collins, "Descendents of Robert Green and Allied Families in the State of Virginia," *Virginia Magazine of History and Biography* 8, no. 1 (July 1900): 77.
31. "Instructions to Lieutenant Colonel John Green, 18 October 1777," Founders Online, https://founders.archives.gov.
32. Heitman, *Historical Register*, 142.
33. Sellers, "Virginia Continental Line," 231, 275.
34. James McMichael, "Diary of Lieutenant James McMichael, of the Pennsylvania Line, 1776–1778," *Pennsylvania Magazine of History and Biography* 16, no. 2 (1892): 153.
35. Sellers, "Virginia Continental Line," 231.
36. Muhlenberg, *Life of Major General Muhlenberg*, 374.
37. Ibid., 211.
38. Ibid., 243.
39. Ibid., 308.
40. Ibid., 243.
41. Marshall Wingfield, *A History of Caroline County, Virginia* (Trevvet Christian, 1924), 39.
42. Heitman, *Historical Register*, 280.
43. Ibid., 448.
44. "To Thomas Jefferson from Sampson Mathews, 13 January 1781," Founders Online, https://founders.archives.gov.
45. *Orderly Book of Captain Robert Gamble* (Virginia Historical Society, 1892), 264–72.
46. Ibid.
47. Heitman, *Historical Register*, 141.
48. Ibid., 260.
49. Conway Oldham to William Davies, March 22, 1781, Executive Papers of Thomas Jefferson, Library of Virginia.

50. "From Thomas Jefferson to James Wood, 17 May 1780," Founders Online, https://founders.archives.gov.
51. "Horatio Gates to Abraham Buford, September 1, 1780," Library of Congress.
52. John R. Van Atta, "Conscription in Revolutionary Virginia: The Case of Culpeper County, 1780–1781," *Virginia Magazine of History and Biography* vol. 92, no. 3 (July 1984), 263.
53. James McDade Pension, S38193, SCAR Pensions and Rosters.
54. Samuel Burke Bounty Land Records, http://revwarapps.org/VAS2789.pdf.
55. *A Size Roll of Noncommissioned Officers and Privates of the Virginia Line*, page 7, SCAR Pensions and Rosters.
56. John Fram Pension, S41526, SCAR Pensions and Rosters.
57. *Size Roll of Noncommissioned Officers and Privates of the Virginia Line*, page 31, SCAR Pensions and Rosters.
58. Moses Rollins Pension, W10241, SCAR Pensions and Rosters.
59. Asher Crockett Pension, W2533, SCAR Pensions and Rosters.
60. Tapley Lightfoot Pension, S4558, SCAR Pensions and Rosters.
61. John Redinhour Pension, S388329, SCAR Pensions and Rosters.
62. Humphrey Hill Pension, S5530, SCAR Pensions and Rosters.
63. Achilles Hoskins Pension, S1218, SCAR Pensions and Rosters.
64. Edward Greenelsh Pension, S5209, SCAR Pensions and Rosters.
65. William Dennis Pension, S39433, SCAR Pensions and Rosters.
66. William Higgins Pension, S16155, SCAR Pensions and Rosters
67. John Foster Pension, S8504, SCAR Pensions and Rosters.
68. "To George Washington from Friedrich Wilhelm Ludolf Gerhard Augustin, Baron [von] Steuben, 23 May 1781," Founders Online, https://founders.archives.gov.
69. *A Size Roll of Noncommissioned Officers and Privates of Virginia*, page 97, SCAR Pensions and Rosters.
70. Ibid., 91.
71. Ibid., 45.
72. *Chesterfield Size Roll*, page 58, SCAR Pensions and Rosters.
73. *A Size Roll of Noncommissioned Officers and Privates of Virginia*, page 31, SCAR Pensions and Rosters.
74. *Chesterfield Size Roll*, page 31, SCAR Pensions and Rosters.
75. *A Size Roll of Noncommissioned Officers and Privates of Virginia*, page 27, SCAR Pensions and Rosters.
76. William Waller Hening, *Hening's Statutes at Large*, vol. 9 (J&G Cochran, 1821), 81.
77. Letter by anonymous staff officer with Burgoyne's Convention Army from Kinderhook, New York, December 18, 1777, in *Letters from America 1776–1779: Being Letters of Brunswick, Hessian, and Waldeck Officers with the British Armies During the Revolution*, edited and translated by Ray W. Pettengill (Kennikat Press, 1964), 119.
78. John U. Rees, *They Were Good Soldiers: African-Americans Serving in the Continental Army, 1775–1783* (Helion, 2019), 37.
79. *A Size Roll of Noncommissioned Officers and Privates of Virginia*, page 25, SCAR Pensions and Rosters.
80. Ibid., page 53.

## *Chapter 2*

81. "To George Washington from Joseph Jones, 11 August 1777," Founders Online, https://founders.archives.gov.

82. "From George Washington to Patrick Henry, 13 November 1777," Founders Online, https://founders.archives.gov.
83. Hening, *Hening's Statutes at Large*, vol. 10, 221.
84. Ibid., 257.
85. Ibid., 258.
86. Ibid., 261–62.
87. Ibid., 259.
88. Ibid., 326–27.
89. Ibid., 331.
90. Ibid., 333.
91. "Petition by the Men of the Amherst County, Virginia Militia Who Fought at the Battle of Camden," Library of Virginia, Legislative Petitions, Reel 9, Box 11, Folder 24, Amherst County
92. "To George Washington from Brigadier General Peter Muhlenberg, 19 June 1780," Founders Online, https://founders.archives.gov.
93. "Thomas Posey, Staunton, to Col. William Davies, 1781 May 18," Library of Virginia.
94. "To Thomas Jefferson from Thomas Gaskins, 23 February 1781," Founders Online, https://founders.archives.gov.
95. Heitman, *Historical Register*, 308.
96. Edwin Hull Pension, W14316, SCAR Pensions and Rosters.
97. Ibid.
98. "To Thomas Jefferson from Thomas Gaskins, 23 February 1781," Founders Online, https://founders.archives.gov.
99. Ibid.
100. "Estimate of Militia Strength [ca. 4 September 1780]," Founders Online, https://founders.archives.gov.
101. Levi Annis Pension, W5624; George Matthews Pension, S38179; Peter Taylor Pension, W6239; James Cropper Pension, S39383; Meshack Waterfield Pension, S38454, SCAR Pensions and Rosters.
102. "To Thomas Jefferson from the Commissioners for Collecting Taxes in Accomac County, 15 May 1781," Founders Online, https://founders.archives.gov.
103. Ibid.
104. "To Thomas Jefferson from George Corbin, 31 May 1781," Founders Online, https://founders.archives.gov.
105. Ibid.
106. "To Thomas Jefferson from Littleberry Mosby, 24 February 1781," Founders Online, https://founders.archives.gov.
107. "To Thomas Jefferson from Littleberry Mosby, 20 April 1781," Founders Online, https://founders.archives.gov.
108. "From George Washington to Samuel Huntington, 10–11 December 1779," Founders Online, https://founders.archives.gov.
109. "From George Washington to Major General Benjamin Lincoln, 12 December 1779," Founders Online, https://founders.archives.gov.
110. Elliott Rucker Pension, S408, SCAR Pensions and Rosters.
111. "From Thomas Jefferson to J. P. G. Muhlenberg, 12 April 1780," Founders Online, https://founders.archives.gov.
112. "To George Washington from Brigadier General Peter Muhlenberg, 8 May 1780," Founders Online, https://founders.archives.gov.
113. "To George Washington from Brigadier General Peter Muhlenberg, 19 June 1780," Founders Online, https://founders.archives.gov.

114. Henry Augustus Philip Muhlenberg (Committee on Revolutionary Claims), "Rep. No. 113," December 22, 1837, https://www.govinfo.gov/content/pkg/SERIALSET-00333_00_00-114-0113-0000/pdf/SERIALSET-00333_00_00-114-0113-0000.pdf.
115. "From Thomas Jefferson to George Gibson, 7 July 1780," Founders Online, https://founders.archives.gov.
116. "From Thomas Jefferson to George Gibson, 14 August 1780," Founders Online, https://founders.archives.gov.
117. Mike Cecere, *An Officer of Very Extraordinary Merit: Charles Porterfield and the American War for Independence* (Heritage Books, 2007), 5.
118. Ibid., 60.
119. Ibid., 108; Sanchez-Saavedra, *Guide*, 122; Public Store Records, Williamsburg, Virginia, May 10, 1779, John D. Rockefeller Library, Colonial Williamsburg Foundation.
120. "Virginia Militia, May 2, 1780, Report on Southern Detachment," Papers of Thomas Jefferson, Library of Congress, https://www.loc.gov/resource/mtj1.002_0049_0049.

## *Chapter 3*

121. "To George Washington from Brigadier General Peter Muhlenberg, 24 February 1780," Founders Online, https://founders.archives.gov.
122. "From George Washington to Brigadier General Peter Muhlenberg, 20 April 1780," Founders Online, https://founders.archives.gov.
123. Ibid.
124. "To George Washington from Brigadier General Peter Muhlenberg, 8 May 1780," Founders Online, https://founders.archives.gov.
125. Ibid.
126. Ibid.
127. "To George Washington from Brigadier General Peter Muhlenberg, 23 May 1780," Founders Online, https://founders.archives.gov.
128. "To George Washington from Brigadier General Peter Muhlenberg, 19 June 1780," Founders Online, https://founders.archives.gov.
129. Ibid.
130. Ibid.
131. Muhlenberg, *Life of Major General Muhlenberg*, 197.
132. "George Washington to Peter Muhlenberg, July 18, 1780," Founders Online, https://founders.archives.gov.
133. Ibid.
134. "To George Washington from Major General Johann Kalb, 29 June 1780," Founders Online, https://founders.archives.gov.
135. Asher Crockett Pension, W5233, SCAR Pensions and Rosters.
136. *Journals of the Council of the State of Virginia*, vol. 2, edited by H.R. McIlwaine (Virginia State Library, 1931), 261.
137. Ibid., 267.
138. "To Thomas Jefferson from Horatio Gates, 21 July 1780," Founders Online, https://founders.archives.gov.
139. Ibid.
140. "To George Washington from Brigadier General Peter Muhlenberg, 24 August 1780," Founders Online, https://founders.archives.gov.
141. "From Thomas Jefferson to Horatio Gates, 4 August 1780," Founders Online, https://founders.archives.gov.

142. Andrew Keyser Pension, S5651, SCAR Pensions and Rosters.
143. Isaac Garvin Pension, W8837, SCAR Pensions and Rosters.
144. Samuel Harris Pension, S10813, SCAR Pensions and Rosters.
145. "To Thomas Jefferson from Horatio Gates, 9 September 1780," Founders Online, https://founders.archives.gov.
146. "To Thomas Jefferson from Horatio Gates, 6 October 1780," Founders Online, https://founders.archives.gov.
147. Moses Rollins Pension, W10241, SCAR Pensions and Rosters.
148. "From Thomas Jefferson to Horatio Gates, 23 September 1780," Founders Online, https://founders.archives.gov.
149. "To Thomas Jefferson from Horatio Gates, 20 September 1780," Founders Online, https://founders.archives.gov.
150. William Dennis Pension, S39433, SCAR Pensions and Rosters.
151. Muhlenberg, *Life of Major General Muhlenberg*, 376.
152. Selby, *Revolution in Virginia*, 216.
153. Muhlenberg, *Life of Major General Muhlenberg*, 207.
154. Ibid., 210.
155. "From George Washington to Major General Nathanael Greene, 14 October 1780," Founders Online, https://founders.archives.gov.
156. "To George Washington from Major General Nathanael Greene, 19 November 1780," Founders Online, https://founders.archives.gov.
157. Ibid.
158. "To Thomas Jefferson from Nathanael Greene, 20 November 1780," Founders Online, https://founders.archives.gov.
159. "To Thomas Jefferson from Nathanael Greene, 6 December 1780," Founders Online, https://founders.archives.gov.
160. Ibid.
161. Edward Sims Pension, S46524, SCAR Pensions and Rosters.
162. "To Thomas Jefferson from Steuben, 10 December 1780," Founders Online, https://founders.archives.gov.
163. "To Thomas Jefferson from Steuben, 15 December [1780]," Founders Online, https://founders.archives.gov.
164. *Chesterfield Size Roll*, page 70, SCAR Pensions and Rosters.
165. Ibid.

## *Chapter 4*

166. Lawrence E. Babits, *A Devil of a Whipping: The Battle of Cowpens* (University of North Carolina Press, 1998), 5.
167. Ibid., 7.
168. Andrew Wallace Bounty Land Warrant, BLWt543-300, SCAR Pensions and Rosters.
169. Joseph A. Waddell, *Annals of Augusta County, Virginia from 1726 to 1871* (C. Russell Caldwell, 1902), 448.
170. John Eager Howard to John Marshall, 1804, Bayard Papers, Maryland Center for History and Culture, Baltimore, Maryland.
171. Henry Emerson Pension, W4949, SCAR Pensions and Rosters.
172. Babits, *Devil of a Whipping*, 55.
173. William Jewell Pension, W11946, SCAR Pensions and Rosters.
174. Robert Owls Pension, S36713, SCAR Pensions and Rosters.

175. Babits, *Devil of a Whipping*, 76.
176. Ibid., 89.
177. Ibid., 100.
178. Ibid., 100.
179. *Pennsylvania Packet*, untitled article, February 18, 1781.
180. John Eager Howard to John Marshall, 1804, Bayard Papers.
181. Babits, *Devil of a Whipping*, 111.
182. John Brownlee Pension, S35799, SCAR Pensions and Rosters.
183. Thomas Crawford Pension, S42147, SCAR Pensions and Rosters
184. William Warren Pension, S11838, SCAR Pensions and Rosters.
185. William Robertson Pension, W2668, SCAR Pensions and Rosters.
186. Isacc Bullin Pension, W5962, SCAR Pensions and Rosters.
187. "Captain Samuel Lapsley to General Nathanael Greene, January 17, 1781," in *Papers of Nathanael Greene*, edited by Richard K. Showman, Dennis Conrad and Roger N. Parks (University of North Carolina Press, 2015), 7:139; "Captain Thomas Bell to General Nathanael Greene, January 21, 1781," in *Papers of Nathanael Greene*, 7:165.
188. *Papers of Nathanael Greene* 7:139–40, 165–66, 169.
189. Lawrence E. Babits and Joshua B. Howard, *Long, Obstinate, and Bloody: The Battle of Guilford Courthouse* (University of North Carolina Press, 2009), 29; Alexander Stewart Pension, W8763; John Winn Pension, S7899.
190. Babits and Howard, *Long, Obstinate, and Bloody*, 35.
191. "To Thomas Jefferson from Steuben 16 December 1780," Founders Online, https://founders.archives.gov.
192. "To George Washington from Major General Steuben 17 December 1780," Founders Online, https://founders.archives.gov.
193. "To George Washington from Major General Steuben 28 December 1780," Founders Online, https://founders.archives.gov.
194. William B. Willcox, ed., *The American Rebellion: Sir Henry Clinton's Narrative of His Campaigns, 1775–1782* (Yale University, 1954), 234.
195. Michael Cecere, *A Universal Appearance of War: The Revolutionary War in Virginia, 1775–1781* (Heritage Books, 2014), 185–86.
196. "From Thomas Jefferson to the County Lieutenants of Charlotte and Certain Other Counties, 2 January 1781," Founders Online, https://founders.archives.gov.
197. "From Baron Steuben to General Nathanael Greene, January 8, 1781," *Papers of Nathanael Greene*, 7:76.
198. Ibid., 77.
199. "From Baron Steuben to General Nathanael Greene, January 8, 1781," in *Papers of Nathanael Greene*, 7:78.
200. Tapley Lightfoot Pension, S4558, SCAR Pensions and Rosters.
201. John Carson Pension, S32167, SCAR Pensions and Rosters.
202. James Slaton Pension, W9655, SCAR Pensions and Rosters.
203. William Loyd Pension, S38145, SCAR Pensions and Rosters.
204. Ephraim Lands Pension, W4066, SCAR Pensions and Rosters.
205. William Seymour, "Journal of the Southern Expedition, 1780–1783, by William Seymour, Sergeant-Major of the Delaware Regiment," *Pennsylvania Magazine of History and Biography* 7 (1883): 378.
206. "George Washington Papers, Series 4, General Correspondence: Nathanael Greene, March 13, 1781, Southern Army," Library of Congress, https://www.loc.gov.
207. Ibid.

208. Ibid.
209. Rev. William Henry Foote, ed., *Sketches of Virginia, Historical and Biographical* (William S. Martein, 1850), 147.
210. Seymour, "Journal of the Southern Expedition," 378.
211. Alexander Stewart Pension, W8763, SCAR Pensions and Rosters.
212. St. George Tucker, "The Southern Campaign 1781 from Guilford Courthouse to the Siege of York," edited by Charles Washington Coleman, *Magazine of American History* 7 (1881): 41.
213. Lewis Griffin Pension, S21248, SCAR Pensions and Rosters.
214. Blackwell P. Robinson, ed., *The Revolutionary War Sketches of William R. Davie* (North Carolina Department of Cultural Resources, 1976), 33
215. Lewis Griffin Pension, S21248, SCAR Pensions and Rosters.
216. Seymour, "Journal of the Southern Expedition," 378.
217. Edward Moody Pension, W2156, SCAR Pensions and Rosters.
218. "To Thomas Jefferson from Charles Magill, 16 March 1781," Founders Online, https://founders.archives.gov.
219. St. George Tucker, "Southern Campaign 1781," 41
220. Robert Clark Pension, S1752, SCAR Pensions and Rosters.
221. Rawleigh C. Christian Pension, W18892, SCAR Pensions and Rosters.
222. Joseph Monk Pension, S38237, SCAR Pensions and Rosters; Christopher McCannon Pension, X897, SCAR Pensions and Rosters.
223. "To Thomas Jefferson from Charles Magill, 16 March 1781," Founders Online, https://founders.archives.gov.
224. Babits and Howard, *Long, Obstinate, and Bloody*, 173.
225. Ibid., 175.
226. "To Thomas Jefferson from Nathanael Greene 27 March 1781," Founders Online, https://founders.archives.gov.
227. "To Thomas Jefferson from Charles Magill, 16 March 1781," Founders Online, https://founders.archives.gov.
228. "General Orders, April 4, 1781," Orderly Book of Nathanael Greene, April 1–July 25, 1781, Manuscripts, Huntington Digital Library.
229. Ibid.
230. John Powell Pension, S38312, SCAR Pensions and Rosters; John Vickers Pension, R10942, SCAR Pensions and Rosters; John Lee Pension, VAS871, SCAR Pensions and Rosters.

## *Chapter 5*

231. "To George Washington from Brigadier General George Weedon, 13 April 1778," Founders Online, https://founders.archives.gov.
232. "From George Washington to Samuel Huntington, 18 June 1780," Founders Online, https://founders.archives.gov.
233. "From Thomas Jefferson to George Weedon 22 October 1780," Founders Online, https://founders.archives.gov.
234. "To George Washington from William Davies, 20 February 1781," Founders Online, https://founders.archives.gov.
235. Ibid.
236. "General Steuben to General Greene, March 30, 1781," in *Papers of General Greene*, 7:15.

237. "To Thomas Jefferson from Steuben [21 April 1781]," Founders Online, https://founders.archives.gov.
238. William Chandler Pension, R1852, SCAR Pensions and Rosters; Thomas Groves Pension, W4211, SCAR Pensions and Rosters.
239. Abner Gordon Pension, S8859, SCAR Pensions and Rosters.
240. Jeremiah Haden Pension, W2107, SCAR Pensions and Rosters.
241. George Connolly Pension, S16734, SCAR Pensions and Rosters.
242. William Garrand Pension, S13122, SCAR Pensions and Rosters.
243. "General Steuben to General Greene, May 15, 1781," in *Papers of General Greene* 7:267.
244. Robert C. Bush III, "The End of Colonel Gaskins' War, May–October 1781," *Bulletin of the Northumberland County Historical Society* 33 (1996).
245. "From Richard Claiborne, Enclosing a List of Articles to Be Furnished to Steuben and Lafayette, 18 May 1781," Founders Online, https://founders.archives.gov.
246. Danske Dandridge, *Historic Shepherdstown* (Michie, 1910), 217–20.
247. Ibid.
248. Ibid.
249. Stanley J. Idzerda, ed., "General LaFayette to General Greene, 18 May, 1781," in *LaFayette in the Age of the American Revolution* (Cornell University Press, 1981), 4:104.
250. William Sutton Pension, S11495, SCAR Pensions and Rosters.
251. Paul Lockhart, *The Drillmaster of Valley Forge: The Baron de Steuben and the Making of the American Army* (HarperCollins, 2008), 261.
252. Banastre Tarleton, "Earl Cornwallis to Sir Henry Clinton, 26 May, 1781," in *A History of the Campaigns of 1780 and 1781 in the Southern Provinces of North America* (Colles, Exhaw, White, H. Whitstone, Burton, Byrne, Moore, Jones and Dornin, 1787), 343.
253. Ibid., 305.
254. Ibid.
255. John Graves Simcoe, *Simcoe's Military Journal* (Bartlett and Welford, 1844), 212–13.
256. Ibid., 214.
257. "Steuben to the Speaker of the Senate [3 June 1781]," Founders Online, https://founders.archives.gov.
258. Ibid.
259. William Sutton Pension, S11495, SCAR Pensions and Rosters.
260. William Tracey Pension, W6307, SCAR Pensions and Rosters.
261. James Slaton Pension, W9655, SCAR Pensions and Rosters.
262. Lockhart, *Drillmaster of Valley Forge*, 264.
263. William White Pension, S1735, SCAR Pensions and Rosters.
264. Receipt, June 8, 1781, Steuben Papers, New York Historical Society.
265. "List of Deserters," June 12, 1781, Steuben Papers, New York Historical Society.
266. David Buffington Pension, W4906, SCAR Pensions and Rosters.
267. Simcoe, *Simcoe's Military Journal*, 223.
268. "To George Washington from Marie-Joseph-Paul-Yves-Roch-Gilbert du Motier, Marquis de Lafayette, 28 June 1781," Founders Online, https://founders.archives.gov.
269. "To Thomas Jefferson from Richard Campbell, 3 April 1781," Founders Online, https://founders.archives.gov.
270. Reuben Long Pension, S46457, SCAR Pensions and Rosters.
271. Ibid.
272. John Dinwiddie Pension, W8671, SCAR Pensions and Rosters.
273. Robert L. Tait Pension, W1330, SCAR Pensions and Rosters.
274. Seymour, "Journal of the Southern Expedition," 381.

275. John Carson Pension, S32167, SCAR Pensions and Rosters.
276. "George Washington Papers, Series 4, General Correspondence: Nathanael Greene to George Washington, April 26, 1781, Return on Southern Army," Library of Congress, https://www.loc.gov.
277. John Carson Pension, S32167, SCAR Pensions and Rosters.
278. "General Greene to Samuel Huntington, President of the Continental Congress, April 26, 1781," in *Papers of General Nathanael Greene*, 7:155.
279. Ibid., 156.
280. Ibid., 156.
281. Guilford Dudley Pension, W8681, SCAR Pensions and Rosters.
282. Edward Moody Pension, W2156, SCAR Pensions and Rosters.
283. "George Washington Papers, Series 4, General Correspondence: Nathanael Greene to George Washington, April 26, 1781, Return on Southern Army," Library of Congress, https://www.loc.gov.
284. Isaac Stephens Pension, W8767, SCAR Pensions and Rosters.
285. John Fryer Pension, S6866, SCAR Pensions and Rosters.
286. James Lewis Pension, S35520, SCAR Pensions and Rosters.
287. "General Greene to the Chevalier de La Luzerne, April 28, 1781," in *Papers of General Nathanael Greene* 7:168.
288. Orders, April 26, 1781, Greene Orderly Book, Huntington Library.
289. Orders, April 30, 1781, Greene Orderly Book, Huntington Library.
290. Orders, May 7, 1781, Greene Orderly Book, Huntington Library.
291. Orders, May 18, 1781, Greene Orderly Book, Huntington Library.
292. Orders, May 28, 1781, Greene Orderly Book, Huntington Library.
293. David Wegar Pension, S15698, SCAR Pensions and Rosters.
294. Bartholomew Cyrus Pension, W25467, SCAR Pensions and Rosters.
295. Edward Sims Pension, S46524, SCAR Pensions and Rosters.
296. "General Greene to Samuel Huntington, President of the Continental Congress, June 20, 1781," in *Papers of Nathanael Greene* 7:419–20.
297. "George Washington Papers, Series 4, General Correspondence: Nathanael Greene to George Washington, April 26, 1781, Return on Southern Army," Library of Congress, https://www.loc.gov.
298. Chapman Poindexter Pension, W26327, SCAR Pensions and Rosters.
299. Thomas Purdom Pension, S38321, SCAR Pensions and Rosters.
300. Edward Nunnelly Pension, W176, SCAR Pensions and Rosters.
301. Chapman Poindexter Pension, W26327, SCAR Pensions and Rosters.
302. Robert E. Lee, ed., *Memoirs of the War in the Southern Department of the United States* (University Publishing Company, 1870), 386–87.

## *Chapter 6*

303. Henry P. Johnston, "Christian Febiger," *Magazine of American History* 6 (1881): 55.
304. "Christian Febiger, Camp, [to] Colonel William Davies," June 30, 1781, Library of Virginia.
305. "Lieut. Col. John F. Mercer to Colo. Simms," in *Fragments of Revolutionary History*, by Gaillard Hunt (Historical Printing Club, 1892), 29.
306. George Johnston Pension, S38088, SCAR Pensions and Rosters; William White Pension, S36107, SCAR Pensions and Rosters.
307. James Slaton Pension, W9655, SCAR Pensions and Rosters.
308. Christian Peters Pension, S5898, SCAR Pensions and Rosters.

309. Thomas Lewis Pension, S7138, SCAR Pensions and Rosters.
310. Charles McMinnis Pension, S36107, SCAR Pensions and Rosters.
311. James Slaton Pension, W9655, SCAR Pensions and Rosters.
312. "General LaFayette to General Washington, July 20, 1781," in *LaFayette in the Age of the American Revolution* 4:256.
313. Anthony Wayne to Thomas Nelson, July 23, 1881, Anthony Wayne Papers, Historical Society of Pennsylvania.
314. John Davis and Jos. A. Waddell, "Diary of Capt. John Davis, of the Pennsylvania Line," *Virginia Magazine of History and Biography* 1, no. 1 (1893): 8.
315. "General LaFayette to General Washington, August 11, 1781," in *LaFayette in the Age of the American Revolution*, 4:312.
316. William Feltmen, *The Journal of Lieut. William Feltmen, of the First Pennsylvania Regiment* (Historical Society of Pennsylvania, 1853), 10.
317. Wayne to Lafayette, August 17, 1781, Anthony Wayne Papers.
318. Flanders Thompson Pension, W6272, SCAR Pensions and Rosters; John Hackett Pension, S37979, SCAR Pensions and Rosters; James Walden Pension, S31454, SCAR Pensions and Rosters.
319. "To George Washington from Friedrich Wilhelm Ludolf Gerhard Augustin, Baron [von] Steuben, 22 October 1781," Founders Online, https://founders.archives.gov.
320. Lafayette to Wayne, August 16, 1781, Anthony Wayne Papers.
321. "General Greene to Governor Thomas Burke of North Carolina, July 16, 1781," in *Papers of General Nathanael Greene*, ed. Dennis M. Conrad, Roger N. Parks and Martha J. King (University of North Carolina Press, 1997), 9:20.
322. "Orders, July 17, 1781," Greene Orderly Book, Huntington Library.
323. "Orders, July 21, 1781," Greene Orderly Book, Huntington Library.
324. "Orders, July 25, 1781," Greene Orderly Book, Huntington Library.
325. "Orders, July 19, 1781," Greene Orderly Book, Huntington Library.
326. "George Washington Papers, Series 4, General Correspondence: Otho H. Williams, Return on Southern Army Infantry Serving under General Nathanael Greene, July 26, 1781," Library of Congress, https://www.loc.gov.
327. Robert M. Dunkerly and Irene B. Boland, *Eutaw Springs: The Final Battle of the American Revolution's Southern Campaign* (University of South Carolina Press, 2017), 23–24.
328. Ibid., 35.
329. Ibid., 112.
330. "General Green to Thomas McKean, President of the Continental Congress, September 11, 1781," in *Papers of General Nathanael Greene*, 9:329.
331. David Wegar Pension, S15698, SCAR Pensions and Rosters.
332. Otho Holland Williams, "Battle of Eutaw," in *Documentary History of the American Revolution* [...] *Chiefly in South Carolina*, edited by R.W. Gibbes (Banner Steam-Power Press, 1853), 3:152, 149
333. "General Green to Thoams McKean, President of the Continental Congress, September 11, 1781," in *Papers of General Nathanael Greene*, 9:329.
334. Williams, "Battle of Eutaw," 150.
335. Lee, *Memoirs of the War*, 471–72; William Davis Pension, S3257, SCAR Pensions and Rosters.
336. Williams, "Battle of Eutaw," 152–53.
337. Ibid., 150.
338. Dunkerly and Boland, *Eutaw Springs*, 92.
339. Williams, "Battle of Eutaw," 153.
340. Tapley Lightfoot Pension, S4558, SCAR Pensions and Rosters.

341. Seymour, "Journal of the Southern Expedition," 387.
342. Ibid.
343. Conrad, "General Green to Thoams McKean, President of the Continental Congress, September 11, 1781," in *Papers of General Nathanael Greene*, 9:331.
344. Lee, *Memoirs of the War*, 473.
345. Ibid.
346. John Wilson Pension Records, VAS1719 and blwt1626-200, SCAR Pensions and Rosters.
347. William Freehold Pension, S42730, SCAR Pensions and Rosters.
348. Charles Clements Pension, S8214, SCAR Pensions and Rosters.
349. Richard Joy Pension, S25182, SCAR Pensions and Rosters.
350. Robert Owls Pension, S36713, SCAR Pensions and Rosters.
351. Gabriel Murphey Pension, S35531, SCAR Pensions and Rosters.
352. Matthew Cummings Pension, S35870, SCAR Pensions and Rosters.
353. William Johnson Pension, W24, SCAR Pensions and Rosters.
354. John Palmer Pension, S8928, SCAR Pensions and Rosters.
355. Edward M. Riley, "St. George Tucker's Journal of the Siege of Yorktown, 1781," *William and Mary Quarterly*, 3rd ser. 5 (1948): 377.
356. Reuben Brizendine Pension, S6754, SCAR Pensions and Rosters.
357. George Booker Pension, S16054, SCAR Pensions and Rosters.
358. H.R. McIlwaine, *Official Letters of the Governor of the State of Virginia* (Virginia State Library 1929), 3:73.
359. "Inspection Return," September 25, 1781, Steuben Papers.
360. James M. Marshall Pension, S7173, SCAR Pensions and Rosters.
361. "Inspection Return," September 25, 1781, Steuben Papers.
362. "General Orders," October 10, 1781, *The Writings of George Washington* (United States Government Printing Office, 1937), 23: 204–5.
363. Philip King Pension, R5961, SCAR Pensions and Rosters.
364. Edward Barker Pension, R496, SCAR Pensions and Rosters.
365. John Davis Pension, S30371, SCAR Pensions and Rosters.
366. Robert Bradshaw Pension, S6708, SCAR Pensions and Rosters.
367. Philip King Pension, R5961, SCAR Pensions and Rosters.
368. William Candler Pension, S9159, SCAR Pensions and Rosters.

## *Chapter 7*

369. "Christian Febiger to George Washington, September 7, 1781," Founders Online, https://founders.archives.gov.
370. Ibid.
371. "To George Washington from Friedrich Wilhelm Ludolf Gerhard Augustin, Baron [von] Steuben, 22 October 1781," Founders Online, https://founders.archives.gov.
372. Ibid.
373. John Davis Pension, S30371, SCAR Pensions and Rosters; John Morgan Pension, S21383, SCAR Pensions and Rosters; William Higgins Pension, S16155, SCAR Pensions and Rosters.
374. Samuel Earle Pension, W7065, SCAR Pensions and Rosters.
375. "Colonel Christian Febiger to Colonel William Davies, November 6, 1781," in William P. Palmer, *Calendar of Virginia State Papers and Other Manuscripts* (Kraus Reprint Corporation, 1968), 2:583.

376. Christian Febiger, Febiger-Posey Orderly Book, Historical Society of Pennsylvania.
377. "Christian Febiger to George Washington, February 10, 1782," Founders Online, https://founders.archives.gov.
378. Ibid.
379. Febiger, "Orders, November 9, 1781," Febiger-Posey Orderly Book.
380. "Colonel Christian Febiger to Colonel William Davies, November 6, 1781," in *Calendar of Virginia*, edited by William P. Palmer (James E. Goode, 1882), 2:583.
381. "Colonel Christian Febiger to Colonel William Davies, November 17, 1781," in *Calendar of Virginia*, 2:609.
382. Ibid.
383. Ibid.
384. Ibid., 610.
385. "George Washington to Christian Febiger, January 12, 1782," Founders Online, https://founders.archives.gov.
386. "From Ensign Daniel Ball to Captain Nathaniel Pendleton, September 26, 1781," in *Papers of General Nathanael Greene*, 9:398.
387. John Carper Pension, S37825, SCAR Pensions and Rosters.
388. "General Orders, November 6, 1781," in *Papers of General Nathanael Greene*, 9:398.
389. "General Orders, November 30, 1781," in *Papers of General Nathanael Greene*, 9:398.
390. Reuben Stout Pension, S14574, SCAR Pensions and Rosters.
391. "To Thomas McKean, President of the Continental Congress, December 9, 1781," in *Papers of General Nathanael Greene*, ed. Dennis M. Conrad and Richard K. Showman (University of North Carolina Press, 1998), 10:111.
392. "To Thomas McKean, President of the Continental Congress, December 9, 1781," in *Papers of General Nathanael Greene* (University of North Carolina Press, 1998), 10:17–18.
393. Ibid., 18.
394. "To Thomas McKean, President of the Continental Congress, December 9, 1781," in *Papers of General Nathanael Greene*, 10:74.
395. Lt. Ballard Smith's Continental Infantry Company Attached to the 3rd Regiment of Continental Light Dragoons, April–July 1782, B137, SCAR Pensions and Rosters.
396. "General Orders, December 10, 1781," in *Papers of General Nathanael Greene*, 10:25.
397. Samuel Harris Pension, S10813, SCAR Pensions and Rosters.
398. "General Orders, December 31, 1781," in *Papers of General Nathanael Greene*, 10:138.
399. "Major Smith Snead to General Nathanael Greene, January 18, 1782," in *Papers of General Nathanael Greene*, 7:101.
400. "Colonel Christian Febiger to Governor Thomas Nelson, November 16, 1781," *Calendar of Virginia*, 2:602.
401. Febiger, "Orders, November 6, 1781," Febiger-Posey Orderly Book. Richard Neale was also a veteran of the Virginia State Garrison Regiment.
402. Febiger, "Orders, November 30, 1781," Febiger-Posey Orderly Book.
403. Febiger, "Orders, December 17, 1781," Febiger-Posey Orderly Book.
404. Febiger, "Orders, November 16, 1781; November 18, 1781," Febiger-Posey Orderly Book.
405. Febiger, "Orders, February 8, 1782," Febiger-Posey Orderly Book.
406. Febiger, "Orders, December 4, 1781," Febiger-Posey Orderly Book.
407. "Colonel Christian Febiger to Colonel William Davies, January 23, 1782," in *Calendar of Virginia*, edited by William P. Palmer (James E. Goode, 1883), 3:44–45.
408. Ibid.
409. Febiger, "Orders, February 4, 1782; February 10, 1782," Febiger-Posey Orderly Book.

410. "Christian Febiger to George Washington, February 10, 1782," Founders Online, https://founders.archives.gov.
411. Francis J. Brooke, *A Family Narrative, Being the Reminiscences of a Revolutionary Officer* (MacFarlane and Ferguson, 1849), 21.
412. "Colonel Christian Febiger to Colonel William Davies, February 23, 1782," *Calendar of Virginia*, 3:72.
413. Brooke, *Family Narrative*, 21.
414. "Christian Febiger to George Washington, February 10, 1782," Founders Online, https://founders.archives.gov.
415. "To George Washington from Christian Febiger, 14 March 1782," Founders Online, https://founders.archives.gov.
416. Ibid.
417. "Colonel Thoams Posey to General Greene, March 11, 1782," in *Papers of General Nathanael Greene*, 10:484.
418. "General Wayne to General Greene, April 9, 1782," in *Papers of General Nathanael Greene*, ed. Dennis M. Conrad and Roger N. Parks (University of North Carolina Press, 2015), 11:25–26.
419. Lee, *Memoirs of the War*, 432–40.
420. "General Wayne to General Greene, May 24, 1782," in *Papers of General Nathanael Greene*, 11:241–44.
421. Muster Rolls for Col. Thomas Posey's Virginia Battalion, January 1782–May 1783, SCAR Pensions and Rosters.
422. John Mallory Pension, R6845, SCAR Pensions and Rosters.
423. "General Wayne to General Greene, June 24, 1782," in *Papers of General Nathanael Greene*, 11:365.
424. Lee, *Memoirs of the War*, 558–59.
425. Reuben Brizendine Pension, S6754, SCAR Pensions and Rosters.
426. Lee, *Memoirs of the War*, 558–59.
427. William Rhodes Pension, S1324, SCAR Pensions and Rosters.
428. Joseph Watson Pension, S11659, SCAR Pensions and Rosters.
429. Lee, *Memoirs of the Wars*, 559.
430. Muster Rolls for Col. Thomas Posey's Virginia Battalion, January 1782–May 1783, SCAR Pensions and Rosters.
431. Alexander Garden, *Anecdotes of the Revolutionary War in America* (A. E. Miller, 1822), 379.
432. Ibid., 380.
433. Edward Jones Pension, S45872; George Chisham Pension, W8594.
434. John Palmer Pension, S8928, SCAR Pensions and Rosters.
435. Vincent Allen Pension, W9692, SCAR Pensions and Fosters.

## *Chapter 8*

436. Muster Rolls for Col. Thomas Posey's Virginia Battalion, January 1782–May 1783, SCAR Pensions and Rosters.
437. Ibid.
438. Brooke, *Family Narrative*, 27.
439. "From Major Samuel Finley to General Nathanael Greene, April 15, 1783," *Papers of General Nathanael Greene*, 11:613.
440. Ibid.

441. Muster Rolls for Col. Thomas Posey's Virginia Battalion, January 1782–May 1783, SCAR Pensions and Rosters.
442. Brooke, *Family Narrative*, 28.
443. Ibid.
444. Muster Rolls for Col. Thomas Posey's Virginia Battalion, January 1782–May 1783, SCAR Pensions and Rosters.
445. William Cooper Pension, S47186, SCAR Pensions and Rosters; James Kemp Pension, S39804, SCAR Pensions and Rosters.
446. Brooke, *Family Narrative*, 28.
447. Parker Copes Pension, S39350, SCAR Pensions and Rosters.
448. Samuel Baskerville Pension, S45238, SCAR Pensions and Rosters.
449. John Shaver Pension, S36753, SCAR Pensions and Rosters.
450. John Irvine Pension, S39763, SCAR Pensions and Rosters.
451. Oliver Wallace Pension, W22543, SCAR Pensions and Rosters.
452. Samuel Allen Pension, S6484, SCAR Pensions and Rosters.
453. Andrew Keyser Pension, S5651, SCAR Pensions and Rosters.
454. Tapley Lightfoot Pension, S4558, SCAR Pensions and Rosters.
455. James Cox Pension, S2441, SCAR Pensions and Rosters.
456. Lewis Griffin Pension, S21248, SCAR Pensions and Rosters.
457. Ibid.
458. William Evans Pension, S35069, SCAR Pensions and Rosters.
459. James Martin Pension, S31236, SCAR Pensions and Rosters.
460. John Short Pension, S37386, SCAR Pensions and Rosters.
461. Robert Owls Pension, S36713, SCAR Pensions and Rosters.
462. *Journal of the House of Delegates, Year 1784* (Thomas W. White, 1828), 17.
463. Robert Clark Pension, S1752, SCAR Pensions and Rosters.
464. John Huffman Pension, W10132, SCAR Pensions and Rosters.
465. William Foxworthy Pension, W8825, SCAR Pensions and Rosters.
466. Bartholomew Cyrus Pension, W25467, SCAR Pensions and Rosters.
467. "Governor Benjamin Harrison to General Greene, October 11, 1783," *Papers of General Nathanael Greene*, ed. Dennis M. Conrad and Roger N. Parks (University of North Carolina Press, 2015), 12:140.

# INDEX

## A



## B



## C



## D



## F

## G



## H



## J



## K



## L



## M



## P



## R



## S

## V



## W



## Y

# ABOUT THE AUTHOR

Having grown up in the shadows of Thomas Jefferson and James Monroe in central Virginia, John C. Settle has always loved history. Settle graduated from Bridgewater College in 2019 with a BA in history. After working for three years as a historical interpreter at Colonial Williamsburg, Settle went into teaching for Accomack and Powhatan County Schools. He currently teaches U.S. history and civics at Powhatan Middle School in Powhatan, Virginia. He has also written articles for the Fluvanna Historical Society and the Journal of the American Revolution. He currently resides in Powhatan, Virginia.